TELL YOURSELF BETTER STORIES

Find Happiness by Becoming the Author of Your Own Life

BY DORIS HASSLOCHER

DOWNLOAD THE AUDIOBOOK FREE!

READ THIS FIRST

To say thanks for downloading my book, I would like to give you the Audiobook version 100% FREE!

I know you're more likely to finish this book if you have the audiobook. I even narrated the book myself so it will feel like we are having a conversation.

Instead of paying $10-$20 for the audiobook, I'd like to give it to you for free…

www.serenityfreedom.com/better-stories-audio

Tell Yourself Better Stories Doris Hasslocher

Table of Contents

6 **Tell Yourself Better Stories** Doris Hasslocher

Introduction

Do you ever find yourself repeating the same unhelpful behaviours? Do you end up in the same arguments or replaying the same dysfunctional relationships? Do you find yourself thinking "not again" more often than you'd like?

Perhaps life feels hard because you believe the only way to find happiness and fulfilment is to move mountains and slay dragons. Perhaps you feel stuck because you think that to live a life you love you must first complete the daunting tasks of fixing yourself, correcting others and repairing a broken world.

Is there a simpler way?

I started puzzling over these questions from when I was very young. I grew up in French-speaking Switzerland from the age of 3 and it wasn't long before I sensed my family and I were the weirdos. It was the early 60s, everyone in the village was a normal Swiss person with a long history and ancestry of Swiss village life. We were an odd family in that environment, newcomers with seemingly flamboyant habits, foreign accents and strange foods.

My family consisted of a Brazilian man married to an English woman with a shy child, that's me, and a Portuguese nanny. We stood out. It was a lovely village and I have many happy memories of playing outdoors all day with all the local kids, but I was very self conscious of how different we were.

When I turned 5 I don't know if my parents forgot to tell me what school was or if I didn't listen when they did, but when the day arrived to attend school for the first time I was thoroughly bewildered. I watched the other kids run around, boisterously carefree, and watched myself stand on the sidelines, cautious, awkward and feeling like an alien. My teacher, hoping to reassure me, started a conversation. But this only terrified me more and I became paralysed with fear of saying the wrong thing in reply. When my mother arrived at the end of the day to pick me up, the teacher reproached her for not telling her I was mute! Apparently, I hadn't spoken a single word the entire day.

Unwanted and recurring patterns of behaviour and emotion usually begin somewhere. I believe this first day of school was the start of one of mine, although I collected many others along the way. I was so afraid of saying the wrong thing to an adult I had never met in a strange frightening new place that I temporarily lost the power of speech. Thankfully my mutism never returned, but that terror of being in an unknown environment where I appear to be the only one who doesn't know what's going on has engulfed me many times through my life, too many to count.

As I grew up through adolescence and into adulthood, I kept watch and observed many other recurring patterns that were equally unpleasant. I frequently found myself frustrated by the same things, engaged in the same conflicts and repeatedly hindered by the same obstacles. I was puzzled as to why I didn't seem to be learning from my experiences, but merely repeating them.

For instance, I often caught myself surreptitiously attempting to "correct" someone's behaviour I judged to be misguided. I found myself having the same argument with my teenage son that my teenage self used to have with my father. An impulse to find someone to blame and criticise came up every time things didn't go as I wanted. I would often get caught up in a conversation that was all about butting heads about who was "right" even when I could see the topic was not important. I frequently defaulted to experiencing fear, self-pity and extreme sadness whenever I was out of my comfort zone.

Travelling the world, living and working in multiple countries, dabbling in adventures, and becoming a mother, doctor, and health coach — though I had many life experiences, these unwanted, recurring mental, emotional, and behavioural patterns continued to pop up.

They were perplexing, unpleasant and counterproductive. They got in the way of what I wanted to do. They prevented me from being who I was, blanketing me with inhibitions. Sometimes I felt imprisoned by them.

Outwardly I was living a fun and interesting life, yet I frequently experienced bouts of unwarranted hostility, helplessness or grief. I missed out on being present in the moment because I was too busy overthinking all my options and criticising all my actions. I was ashamed of my embarrassing thoughts and feelings, and it was hard work containing all that. It's no wonder I was pretty tense!

As my hindering patterns only gained strength over time, I began to picture a rather bleak future, with me becoming more and more limited. In my more fanciful moments, I saw myself as a crazy old bag lady living under a bridge with all my possessions in a shopping trolley, abandoned by all my friends and relations.

I was able to laugh at my exaggerated doomful vision of my future, and I was able to reassure myself, but daily battling against those patterns of negative thought and emotion was draining. All I could think to do was try harder and push myself to do better, which only exhausted me more.

Have you noticed any patterns in yourself such as this? If you're anything like me perhaps they also frustrate you and get in your way.

As I wrestled with this phenomenon, I noticed that I wasn't alone, that other people appeared to have their own set of sabotaging patterns too. I also noticed another group of people who didn't — people who were free, who achieved the things they wanted without encountering a sea of obstacles, who jumped in with both feet and came up laughing. These people loved life and found everything easy and fun. I wanted to be like them.

I realised that if I wanted to change my life, I had to answer my biggest questions: *Why do I say, do, think and feel things that lead to outcomes I don't want? And how do I stop?*

In an effort to find answers, I dove into every book, teacher, course, workshop, podcast and experience that I thought might shed light on this phenomenon of living a life needlessly filled with obstructive patterns of behaviour, thought and emotion.

Many observations, areas of study and life experiences gradually allowed me to gather a more detailed picture of this strange habit so many of us have of putting obstacles in our own path or getting lost inside our own heads going around in circles.

I was disappointed to find my medical education didn't shed any light on the topic of why many of us think, feel and act in counterproductive ways that create the outcomes we don't want. However, my 35 years as a doctor did serve as a great forum for further observation of human behaviour, including my own.

As a young intern in my first year, I admitted a lovely gentleman to the surgical ward. A few days later the result of the biopsy on his oesophagus came back, showing an early cancer. Oesophageal cancer is frequently diagnosed late and fairly rapidly fatal but my boss, a surgeon with many years of experience told me this was the smallest and earliest oesophageal cancer he had seen in his career; he was enthusiastic as he held out great hopes for a complete cure with surgery. I went to tell my sweet patient the news. He was quiet a few moments and then replied: "So. It is cancer then." I remembered then what he had told me at his admission — that cancer was his greatest fear.

He died 3 days later. The immediate cause of his death wasn't established, but I still remember the resignation on his face as he said those words that confirmed his greatest fear.

I knew I could not draw any conclusions about my patient, but this early and impactful experience did make me wonder about the power of people's beliefs. As I continued to closely observe myself and others, I began to see a strong connection between beliefs formed in the past and life experiences.

I recall the instant irritation I felt as a 30-something living in Sydney when someone told me something clearly untrue because it took me straight back to the frustrating and ridiculous argument I had with another kid when I was 8. When I was unable to master a new software in my 50s, I went into the same cold sweat I'd had in high school when my history teacher left me standing at the front of the class in shame with the question I couldn't answer. I was overcome with that same first-day-at-school terror when I mistakenly walked into the advanced ballerina class instead of hip hop for beginners.

What I realised in my quest for answers was that one of the reasons we habitually repeat unwanted behaviours and encounter the same undesirable scenarios is because, in the background and under the radar, we are running scripts.

My big discovery was simply that at the root of this hindering habit is an underground story that's getting in our way.

These scripts, or stories, were programmed into us long ago. We may be totally unaware of them or all too aware of them, but the scripts run just the same. Yet these scripts are far from immutable. Changing them is a bit like updating the software or editing the words of the playwright.

In the movie *Groundhog Day*, Phil Connors (played by Bill Murray) wakes every morning to discover it's the same day as it was yesterday — and that he has to live it all over again. It takes him a while to get past his frustration, but eventually Phil realises he has the power to respond differently. He gets up every day in the same situation, but he discovers he can change his words and actions. When he finally masters the art of creating a better script, he gets the outcomes his heart desires.

This movie is a reminder that we can get very different results with different inputs. Changing our beliefs, assumptions and attitudes can create an entirely different experience.

Like Phil Connors in *Groundhog Day*, it took me a while to move beyond frustration at this constant replay of well-worn patterns. Little by little I understood that I could alter the outcomes I was seeing in my life by altering my thoughts and my viewpoint, which in turn altered my actions and responses.

When I did, I started to experiment with different ways of thinking. I learned how to reframe my beliefs and develop new thought habits. I began to catch myself just before falling into the same old patterns and diverting into healthier patterns instead.

I didn't get it right straight away, there was a lot of trial and error and sometimes I made things worse. But as I kept practising the strategies I learned, something amazing happened. I began to see some very tangible and gratifying differences not only in the events of my life but also in the ways in which I saw myself and the world in general. Since then, I've helped others to walk this road and learn how to change their stories and seen equally pleasing results as they put the strategies into practice in their own lives.

None of us are doomed to constantly repeat the patterns of our lives. If we want to, we can create new patterns — ones that lead to the outcomes we want, rather than accept, perhaps in resignation and resentment, the outcomes we get by default.

You can evaluate your own scripts — the stories you tell yourself — so you can take charge of your own life. If you feel stuck and frustrated and would like to free yourself from old scripts you didn't even write yourself, to stop repeating tired, overused patterns and create new ones, this book will show you how.

In chapters 1–5 we'll look at this idea of stories or scripts and how they develop in the first place, with examples of how this can play out in people's lives. We'll also examine the cost of running stories that aren't of our own choosing and what can happen to us physically if we continue to do so.

Chapters 6–8 will show you not only that it's entirely possible to replace outdated scripts with better ones, but that doing so is neither complicated nor unattainable. We'll highlight some obstacles that could hold you back in chapters 9–11 and in chapters 12–14 you'll turn theory into reality in creating new scripts that serve you better, gaining a felt experience of the principles in this book and internalising the new understandings so that they "stick" for the long term instead of being forgotten once you put the book down.

Most of us know we sometimes act in ways we'd rather not — and most of us sense those actions can be changed. It's easy to glibly say, as I often have, "I already know that". We already know that our perspective makes a difference to what ends up happening. But it's one thing to know something intellectually, and quite another thing to make it a reality.

This book will help you make it a reality. You can learn how to tell yourself better stories. You can replace old scripts with new ones. You can stop repeatedly living the same unwanted experiences. And you can become the author of your own life.

Chapter 1
Tell Me a Story

From cheerfully pottering about the kitchen on a relaxing day at home, I sat to check some emails, looking forward to reading news from friends and to the satisfying feeling of deleting spam. As I skimmed subject lines and senders my happy flow came to an abrupt halt. A tight knot formed in my gut and my throat clenched. A wave of dread washed over me.

Micro-expressions of fear crossed my face as it changed from relaxed to frowny. My shoulder blades and arms tensed as I unwittingly adopted a self-defence posture. My breath became shallow and moved to the top of my rib cage. Ashamed of my intense response to a mere email I rose, telling myself to act normal, walking about stiffly like a robot, aware of my illogical panic.

In that moment, I saw it: I'd been hooked by a story.

My Eureka Moment

What was in that terrible email on my screen? What was so show-stopping, so earth-shattering? It was my accountant, writing to ask for a couple more details so he could do my tax return. The minute I read this harmless email, covertly in the background, my pre-programmed narrative began, *I haven't got the information he wants. I don't know where it is, it's buried somewhere in my computer, I'll never find it. I don't understand why he's asking. He probably just wants to charge me for more emails. I'm always being ripped off. I feel helpless and stupid again.* And so on and so forth.

Have you ever felt surprisingly disturbed in response to something outwardly trivial?

I realised with a jolt that despite my intense emotions the words I read on the screen had no power to hurt me. I was reacting so strongly to nothing more dangerous than some noughts and zeroes exchanged between two computers in response to hands touching a keyboard. My eureka moment was a realisation.

What stood out in blazing neon lights in my awareness was the moment I caught myself reacting to the email in a way that wasn't natural to me. It was as if the director of my life-movie shouted "Action!" and I switched into being the actor playing a part I had carefully memorised. The changes in my face, body, movements and breathing were not mine, they were my character's.

Contrary to what I had believed my whole life, I suddenly saw that this response was something I was *doing*, not something that was happening to me.

I saw that my response was a choice, albeit unintended. It was a habit. I had simply acquired this habit, based on a story I had been telling for a long time. I saw that it did not have to be this way. This was an immensely liberating realisation!

If this reaction was indeed just a habit I had unconsciously picked up then I could change it. In my flash of comprehension, I saw that the frowny-faced, knotted-up individual wasn't me: it was a role I was playing. I was both the actor and the script-writer. That meant I could stop and walk off the stage.

The Power of Choice

A memory, an event or the sight of something can set off a physical and emotional response inside us. Often, because we have encountered something similar before, we already have a pre-programmed response ready and waiting. We respond to big things, such as loss and injury, and smaller things, such as bills, emails from accountants, rainy weather or a perceived insult and these responses are unique to us, based on our past history.

At various points in our lives, we learned, then practised, responses to common events. We got some from our parents, others from our experiences and it's natural that we created them as they save us time and effort. It would be tiresome to have to re-learn the answer to a simple greeting every time we heard it. However, not all pre-programmed responses are created equal, some are more beneficial than others.

In the movie *Back to The Future*, the spirited young hero Marty McFly had a well-practised, angrily indignant, response to being called "chicken," which happened a number of times. I wonder if you can think of some common knee-jerk responses you may have to certain things being said or done. Most of us have at least one or two buttons that can be pushed by a word or phrase.

What's immensely liberating is understanding that our honed and practised response is only one of many possible options.

In that briefest of moments between an event and our response to it, we do have a choice. We can bypass our usual reaction and select another, if we so wish. Marty McFly's hot-tempered reaction regularly put him in danger. My response to the email, on the other hand, didn't put me in danger, but it did generate some highly unpleasant emotions and sensations for several hours. I'd like to have done something more productive with that time.

Our responses are generally based on an internal narrative, a story we have been telling ourselves. The story started one day and we have told it, or some version of it, many times since. We may barely notice ourselves telling it, it may only run *sotto voce* inside our minds, perhaps even wordlessly, represented only with feelings and images. It's become our default story. It goes unexamined and we enact the prescribed response without question as if that were our one and only option.

Some stories are fun, satisfying, and instructive. Others bring us down and stress us out. If we don't know that we have a choice — that we can walk off the stage or act in a different way— we may typecast ourselves as the characters we sometimes play. We may play the villain or the victim. We may play the rescuer or the misanthrope. At times we may play the helpless child. This wastes a lot of energy in unnecessary turmoil and misery.

The good news is you don't have to live this way. You can start to notice the roles you often play. You can bring your automatic scripts into the light, decide if they lead to sensations and results you enjoy, or sensations and results you'd rather not have. You can select which roles to accept and which to turn down.

It may be challenging at first to uncover the automatic scripts that are running undercover and to distinguish between those that usefully save time and those that lead to angst. It's often easier to see it play out in someone else's life than your own. So let me tell you a story.

Chapter 2
Once Upon A Time

Sarah grew up in Sussex, the only child of immigrants from Europe, loving parents who were nevertheless frequently in some kind of passive-aggressive conflict. Her father was playful and generous, but also moody and tantrum-prone. He could be stormy, judgemental and would badger people into listening to his lectures or batter them with his strong opinions. Sarah's mother came from an affectionate family and had no idea how to deal with this covert bullying, so she resorted to plaintiveness and resentment, which Sarah witnessed daily as she was growing up.

Richard grew up in Wales, descending from Celtic warriors in generations past, where over time the formerly valiant wars had gradually shifted from outside to inside the home. He witnessed a lot of shouting and drama as he grew up and perceived himself to be an unwelcome, troublesome burden to his beleaguered parents. Before long he had only one beleaguered parent, his father having disappeared off the scene without leaving a forwarding address.

Sarah grew up to be a strong-minded young woman with a thirst for new experiences, but this only got her into trouble when it came to romantic relationships. She didn't realise it, but she repeatedly fell in love with men who reminded her of her father and repeatedly dealt with them by emulating her mother.

Richard left his turbulent home almost as soon as he had two digits to his age and joined one institution or group after another, seeking a form of family to belong to where he might be wanted and appreciated.

True Love

When Sarah met Richard, she thought things were going to be very different. Richard was nothing like her previous boyfriends. He was romantic, playful, affectionate, spoke poetic words and excited her more than anyone else had. This felt like the type of love she had seen in movies. Not the mundane everyday boring love, but the thrilling, over-the-rainbow, soul-mate type of love. You know, like in all the songs and romance novels, the happy-ever-after ones. Sarah was sure of it. Even when she sensed unease among her friends she was still sure of it. They rode off into the sunset together. She had found true love.

When Richard met Sarah, he thought she was the feistiest, most adventurous and independent woman he had ever met. His previous girlfriends had been playful enough but seemed quite needy after a short while. He found it rather burdensome to have girlfriends who depended on him for their self-esteem and was somewhat in awe of Sarah who seemed not to need anyone. He boldly expressed his love and admiration, fully prepared for rejection. He was delighted and surprised when Sarah wildly threw her fate in with his, to set off on adventures together. He had found true love.

Very soon, things began to unsettle Sarah. Little things. Things she tried not to notice. Things she excused, or blamed herself for. Very soon, things began to unsettle Richard. He felt a little inadequate, and in his efforts to assert his own needs, he began to find fault with Sarah.

In what seemed like a very short space of time, Sarah found herself bewildered by where she was. Richard, previously so attentive, became aloof and disengaged. He began to disappear, to stay away longer and longer. He began to act surly, unappreciative, entitled and grumpy. He seemed to expect to be treated with deference and he contributed less and less materially. Sarah couldn't understand it. What's more, she had no idea how to respond. So she responded, by default, in the only way that had been modelled for her while she was growing up. Plaintively and resentfully.

In what seemed like a very short period of time, Richard found himself wanting to avoid Sarah without exactly knowing why. He had the vague feeling she didn't appreciate or value him and so he retaliated by finding his fun, conversation and companionship elsewhere. He responded in a way that seemed strangely familiar to him, by becoming absent even when he was physically present, by creating drama and conflict and by engaging in a cold war.

And so began the dance, each one embodying their respective roles to perfection. Neither one liked who they had become, neither one got any benefit beyond fleeting moments of "being right." Sarah believed herself to have the moral high ground, while Richard congratulated himself for being stronger.

Ending The Dance

Richard and Sarah were both besotted with their beautiful baby boy but his arrival did little to change the dance in which they were now solidly engaged. Richard stayed out even more, regularly disappearing for a day or two then sleeping for hours when he did reappear, only to be cantankerous upon awakening. The only time Sarah glimpsed the real Richard was when he lit up in joy at playing with their son.

Sarah retreated into herself more and more, hiding the truth from her friends, nursing her despair, seething with resentment, feeling lonely and hopeless. The only time Richard glimpsed the real Sarah was when, in some brief moment, they found the space to reconnect and be once more who they were at heart.

Sarah was not by nature a victim, any more than Richard was by nature heartless, but they had imbibed these patterns. They had fallen into a rut of repeating the same unhelpful narratives and behaviours while expecting a different outcome to miraculously appear or expecting the change to come from the other person.

Survival instincts took over and the relationship dissolved. The parting was painful and a little messy, but relatively clean compared to some.

Many people have a story like Sarah and Richard. They may not realise that some of their actions, their feelings and their responses are being directed by a script they internalised long ago without knowingly choosing to do so.

Could Sarah and Richard have responded differently to each other or to the events of their lives? Might they have found a longer term happiness together? Or, if parting was indeed their best choice, might they have had an easier parting if they had been able to recognise and modify some of those internal scripts? Might they, once separated, retain a happier memory of their time together and be better prepared for a future romance, had they chosen more deliberately the lens through which to view the memory?

Many of us have a tale about something that didn't go as we'd hoped. How we tell that tale, how we remember it and how we feel towards it can be part of what determines our future. But before we can change our future trajectory, we must first understand how stories are born.

Chapter 3
Where Do Stories Come From?

What is the origin of these stories or scripts we unconsciously adopt and the roles we play out in our lives? Let's go to the beginning.

At birth we have relatively few skills in place. We can't walk or lift our own head. We can't talk and we can't focus very well. We spend years learning all we need to know from the people around us. We see them walk, so we learn to walk. We hear them talk, so we learn to talk. We observe carefully what the rules are, what the consequences are, what happens when. We suck it all up avidly, we are finely tuned learning machines.

Until we are about 6 years old, we have very little, if any, capacity to filter and triage what we witness and learn. We don't question why our parents are speaking Swahili rather than Hungarian, we just learn to speak Swahili. We cannot say to ourselves when we are 4 and our father shouts at us for grabbing at cookies in the supermarket, "Oh, Dad doesn't really think I'm greedy and selfish and I already know I'm not, he's just out of sorts today because that shelf fell on his head and his boss yelled at him."

What parents say or do, how they act, their assumptions, their moods and reactions, all of this is what their children absorb as they grow up. Most of this content is both helpful and necessary. But not all of it.

Some of it may inadvertently hurt, depending on what the child makes of it, with their limited ability to filter. What a parent says during an unguarded moment, especially when it carries a strong emotion, will sink into their children's minds and stay there unless it gets replaced by something else. Even as we mature into adults, the ability to rationalise and filter content is variable. At any age we can let ourselves be hurt by a word or an event if we don't know how to confidently choose our own interpretation and override the previous pattern.

My own father was caring and kind, yet he periodically played another persona when under stress. At those times he emanated a heavy, ominous seriousness, which I unconsciously sensed and absorbed. I also got from him the idea that money was a mysterious, complicated and difficult topic. This may have originated from certain periods in my father's otherwise prosperous life during which he was penniless. The distress and guilt this caused him became part of his fabric, it radiated from him.

Later, as an early teen, I heard of my father's secret fear I would one day marry someone who took advantage of me financially, as happened with a close relative. My fury and indignation at the implied insult to my intelligence did not prevent me from subliminally taking on board the idea that I was congenitally inept at managing money. One day in my young adulthood, I was pleased when my father offered to teach me about stocks and shares, the mysterious pursuit he engaged in which kept us relatively well off. Unfortunately he gave me no context or background and I understood nothing of what he was telling me. With me embarrassed and him discouraged, the topic was never again mentioned. From these experiences I deduced, without realising until much later that I was deducing anything, that money was something I couldn't ever master and that this made me vulnerable. Hence my visceral fear of bills and questions from accountants. I didn't know at the time that I was learning a story and for many years I didn't even know I had this script running in the background. All I knew was bills and accountants made me anxious.

Parents are not the villains: they're humans picking up stories from their environment, just like the rest of us. What they say and do originates from what they witnessed when they were young themselves.

It's the people who are closest to us who influence us the most at first, but they in turn, are influenced by the culture they are in, as we will be too when we begin to venture further from the hearth.

If we grow up in China, we'll learn Chinese fables, linguistic and cultural habits and relationship norms. Growing up in France leads to learning the French equivalents. I learned cultural and linguistic treasures from Switzerland until I was 12 and then switched to English norms at 14, with a two-year gap in

Jakarta where I also picked up a few things. In my case I got to pick up more than one culture's norms, but no matter where someone grows up and lives they will absorb the influences around them.

The individuals who raise us, and later our friends and the culture around us, influence what scripts and stories are available to us to collect. It's not only geographical differences, but also time differences that determine the stories we take on board. Growing up in the 1850s led to learning very different habits and cultural norms than growing up in the 2050s will. Your younger sibling may have gleaned different messages from your parents than you did, because your parents probably had different perspectives by then.

It's not necessarily just the facts of a story that affect us the most. Their emotional content and the assumptions hidden within the story can have the greatest impact. I didn't simply learn that I was judged naive and inept about money, I also learned the fear and helplessness that followed from that opinion of me. I learned that not only was I inept but that this left me at risk and less capable of being all that I might want to be. I learned to be afraid. I learned to keep my expectations low.

Sticky Stories

Stories and scripts come from parents, teachers, the movies and TV shows we watch, the books we read and the tales people tell us. They come from articles, snippets, advertisements and scenes we witness in our day-to-day life. We cobble them together from multiple bits we collect. Then we tell them — to ourselves and to each other.

We don't generally stand up on a stage with a microphone to tell them. Instead we embed them in the images, concepts and assumptions we hold. We tell our stories non-verbally, through our actions and our life-choices. We see and hear them told in our dreams and desires and we also tell them with our words. We repeat them, embellishing and embedding them and much of the time we don't even realise we are acting out stories.

The more you do something, the easier it gets to keep doing it. The more we tell ourselves our stories, the more we act them out, the more we express them to our friends, the easier it gets to keep on doing that. A story we pick up from a chance remark could get forgotten and blown away in the wind. Or it could get repeated, lived, enacted and told until it sticks. This can happen without us being aware of it and without us taking the time to decide if we want it to stick.

For a long time I barely understood that stories were running my life. I simply felt frustrated and stuck in a cycle of repeating unenjoyable experiences and emotions. I blamed others and I blamed my inadequacies and I remained stuck.

As the concept of false assumptions, hindering perceptions and stories began to slowly dawn on me, I started to sense that not all of them were accurate or helpful and that they need not govern my world.

However I didn't see how to disconnect from the stories. Sometimes I tried going directly against them but they played out anyway and sometimes I didn't realise they were playing out until many years later.

For instance, I grew up knowing that my parents worried a lot about me. This may have resulted from the long difficult labour that preceded my arrival, my many mysterious childhood illnesses, my incomprehensible shyness to my maternal line of extroverts and the tendency (or hobby) of certain relatives to avidly collect things to worry about. Whatever the reasons for the worry, what affected me profoundly was that they did worry. I was a child, I never questioned it or understood it. I simply grew up knowing that I was something to worry about.

With no awareness of what was happening, I played the role of being someone people worried about. I saw myself as small, vulnerable and incapable. As I matured I became at least partly aware and tried to rebel. I wanted to change this image of myself. In attempting to reject this story, I regularly pushed myself to actions that were not in my best interests. It was a long time before I understood that openly fighting against the notion that I was weak and incapable was only reinforcing the image I wanted to change. If something is clearly not true, it's irrelevant to you. You don't need to fight against it or prove it wrong, you simply dismiss it and get on with your life.

Step by step over time I taught myself to accept my own capability. This has resulted in a calm self-assurance. It has given me peace from the tiresome work of constantly justifying my existence with exhausting acts designed to demonstrate capability and strength. The best part is that I am doing just as many fun exciting things, if not more, but now I'm doing them for the fun of it, free from any compulsion to prove something about myself.

You Can Choose

Every story, just like every song, carries a particular vibration, a particular energy, a particular bundle of emotions, sensations and thoughts. That bundle has an impact. It can elevate or reduce. It can inspire or disempower. It can be helpful or hurtful. It can affect how you feel every day; it can affect how much you love or don't love life and how your future pans out.

My aim is to show you how to identify which stories are currently guiding you and to help you get better at choosing the good ones and discarding the ones that hold you back. And if you think you don't have that many good ones, you can easily create some.

Our stories, responses, attitudes and opinions can feel permanent, as if they are forever a part of our identity, but they are not. We are almost infinitely adaptable.

You choose what music you listen to and what ice cream flavour you eat — we all have preferences. You don't need to explain your preferences or justify them, and you don't need to keep eating an ice cream flavour you don't like. You don't have to listen to music you don't enjoy. Instead, you can live by stories that carry emotions and outcomes you do want to experience.

Personally, I am rather fond of feeling satisfaction, curiosity, excitement and fun. I also like feeling appreciation, novelty, amusement and energy. It's in my power to create those emotions regardless of the supposed truths of my material life. I can do that by choosing which stories I tell.

Stories aren't bad in and of themselves. They are a part of life. They have been told throughout history since we first sat around campfires. They are told inside ourselves and they are told outwardly. Stories can be fun and helpful; they can also be draining and unhelpful.

The question is whether you're being positively or negatively impacted by them. Are they bringing you joy or grief? If all is well and you love your life, then your stories are serving you well. However, if you're feeling stuck, blocked in your progress and exhausted by draining emotions, then you have the option to let go of overused, unhelpful scripts and replace them with better ones.

As you read, you will start to become more conscious of your own stories. You can write your own history by choosing your stories. You can be the boss of your internal state and of the results you see in your life.

Let's now examine some common stories that are not especially helpful.

Chapter 4
12 Unhelpful Stories

Your life history, your experiences over the years are completely unique to you. Even if you have a twin, there are likely subtle differences in how you were treated and the decisions you made. Like snowflakes, your stories are also unique. Yet underlying all that uniqueness are some common threads.

Among the following sample of stories, some will be familiar to you. You may have seen them in yourself, in others or in movies and books. I have personally dallied with all of them at one time or another, some being more tenacious than others. How active a part each story plays in our life will vary over time, according to what else is going on.

As you go through the descriptions of the thoughts, feelings and behaviours characterising each of these 12 story types, you may start to see that they are different versions of one underlying fundamental story. See what you think that foundational element is, and I will offer what I think it is at the end of the chapter.

1. Proving Worth

I am not worthy or valuable as I am. I must prove my worth. I am of value only when I am visibly helping others, doing good, being successful, performing athletic feats, saving the planet, being the best or sacrificing myself. I often talk about what good deeds I have done and how many people I have helped. I say things like, "I had to go and pick him up at the airport" or "I had to cancel the thing I was doing because she needed me." My words reflect my belief that the needs of someone else should trump mine, though I allow myself to resent them for it.

2. I Don't Belong

I secretly believe I'm different, defective, shameful, abnormal and unacceptable. I crave belonging. I am lonely and fear rejection. The only way I can get love and belonging is by conforming to what the group wants, even if it goes against my own desires, values, beliefs, wishes and preferences. In extreme cases, even if it threatens my life. My need to belong overrides my desire to thrive and follow my dreams. In order to belong, I will change my beliefs, stand up for things I don't truly believe in, eat things I know are not good for me and agree with things I don't really agree with. I privately resent or complain about the group and I may move from one group to another in my search for belonging.

3. Taking on Suffering

I feel other people's feelings. I believe I know how they must feel even when I haven't asked them how they feel. I experience pity, fear, sadness and anger on other people's behalf. I feel sorry for children and animals in particular. I viscerally feel in my own body the misery and suffering I believe them to be experiencing. I often talk about how bad things are, what wrongs are being done. I often use words like sad, awful, terrible, wrong and ghastly, even about trivial things like a rainy day. I feel helpless to act so I take on the emotion myself and carry it like a cross because that makes me feel I am at least doing something to help those who are suffering. I believe my suffering by proxy makes me more virtuous than others who may not notice or seem to care.

4. Fixing What is Broken

I came here to fix things: it's my job. I have to make things right. My biggest problem is that I need others to do things differently and that's hard work. I need to tell them where they are going wrong, point out their mistakes, mould and control them into changing their ways. If I can't accomplish that I will at least feel angry at them, swear at them from behind the wheel of my car, mutter about them under my breath, rant to anyone who will listen about all that they are doing wrong that does not conform to my model of how the world should be.

5. Fixing Myself

I'm broken, I must fix myself in order to be acceptable. I push myself, I work hard, I do what I hate, I explore every avenue compulsively in an attempt to reach my idea of perfection. I don't acknowledge my own successes and achievements. I belittle my progress, because I'm too busy looking to the next level I must now get to, as soon as possible. I attend every workshop, read every book, do every training, try every diet and health hack and see every therapist in my urge to repair what is broken inside me but I never find the right one. I keep seeking, each action inexorably leading to the next.

6. I Must Know

I analyse and evaluate everything. I must understand, I must have the facts and I must give everything a score out of 10 for validity. I must get it right and be right. I'm most satisfied when I give the right answer, when I know things others don't. I'm anxious if I can't understand something or if I feel confused and uncertain. If I find evidence that contradicts what I learned at school or professionally, I feel threatened and reject the new information. The world is only safe if I understand and know everything. If in doubt, I quickly retreat to my mind before I get hurt. I ignore my feelings and mistrust my instincts because they can't be proven, demonstrated and verified. Besides, I can't be admired and respected for them, only for my knowledge and expertise.

7. I Must Keep up

I got here too late. I'm on the back foot. I missed the beginning. I'm coming last in the race. I must hurry, I must run faster, do more. I'm always rushing, I try to get everything done, I keep long lists of what I must do. I get stressed if I think I missed an episode, a chapter or an event. I will try my best to catch up and get up to speed but I always feel I am behind. I need to finish this so I can start that. I already know what I'll be doing next and after that and after that, so I need to get on. I mustn't dawdle nor stop to smell the roses — unless it's on my list, in which case I'll smell them, tick the box and quickly move on to what's next on the list. I hate to leave anything open and unfinished, even if it's just a box of chocolates.

8. I'm Incapable

I fall into self-pity and dwell on the ways in which I have been mistreated or disrespected. I may give up, throw in the towel, resign myself to mediocrity because getting what I want seems too hard. Or I may valiantly try to prove myself strong by telling stories of how "I showed him" and how "I sure put her in her place" and by demonstrating my capabilities. I may rehearse in my mind arguments and debates proving I did the right thing. Or I may switch over to "everyone's an idiot" and berate all the people around me who do "stupid" things. While I may not tell them my opinion I do so in my own mind or to my friends who are willing to listen. Sometimes I act recklessly to prove my strength, to rebel against the feeling that I'm not strong.

9. Deferring to Authority

I don't have permission and I need an authority to tell me what to do. I obey orders. I report to the authorities those who don't obey orders. I don't feel safe unless someone tells me what to do. I am constantly striving to be a good boy or good girl and to get the teacher's praise. I also fear authority. I get nervous if I see a police car, a uniformed official or if I get a letter from the tax office. I hand over my health entirely to experts and believe illness is an attack from outside that must be beaten, overcome and exterminated by an intervention from outside. I do not trust in my own body's capacity to heal itself. I do not trust in my own capacity to achieve the things I want in life. I make choices based on what experts tell me, disregarding my instincts. I read and learn what I'm told to read and learn or what I think others will approve of. I follow instructions to the letter and feel betrayed if I don't get the outcome I was "promised."

10. Saving the Planet

I must be the knight in shining armour. I do good. I recycle. I want people to avoid driving and flying. I believe the planet is fragile and vulnerable, that humans are greedy, evil and a scourge. I must right wrongs, overcome odds. I must save everyone and everything. I feel overwhelmed and despondent at times because my task is too great. It's also confusing. Information is contradictory, so at times I feel paralysed and don't know what to do. At other times, I feel righteously virtuous because I am doing so much to try to save the earth or the whales or the children and others are selfishly not doing the things I'm doing. I feel contempt and impotent anger towards them. I can't rest until I have repaired all the mistakes we have made, but sometimes I'm exhausted and I don't know where to start.

11. The Bad Guys

The world is made of good guys and bad guys. I've researched all about the bad guys, doing bad things, I know all about them. I've joined groups where we discuss them and condemn their actions. Bad guys are rich and powerful, they are cruel and have no souls, they aren't human. I think about them and the terrible things they do. I worry, fear and rage about them. When I look around, I don't see much good. It's hard for me to appreciate beauty and feel light-hearted. I mostly focus on how the evil-doers should be jailed or executed. I feel helpless because I can't get rid of the bad stuff and the government isn't doing its job and most other people don't get it. I don't have much faith in this turning out well, I see the future as dark. Someone should do something.

12. Emotions Are Dangerous

I shove my feelings down. I want them to go away. Feelings are scary, I don't know what to do with them. If I feel upset, I criticise myself or I find who to blame. I don't talk about things that may cause unpleasant emotions. I crave sameness and get my safety from having things stay the same, that way there are fewer feelings to handle. Change is scary and undesirable. I am uneasy with life transitions or with new things. I don't like conflict, I avoid it as much as humanly possible. I'd rather pretend to agree than risk a disagreement. I don't have goals in my life in case they conflict with anyone else's. I won't say what I want because they may refuse or argue and I don't want to experience disappointment, fear or anger. I become voiceless and passive and then I resent others for the things they aren't doing that they should be doing and for not meeting my needs.

Benefits of Better Stories

These 12 stories are not meant as a definitive or an exhaustive list, only examples of some unhelpful patterns I have noticed. There is overlap between them and you can probably think of some different ones. Did you recognise some aspects of these in yourself?

In each of them you probably noticed that there is some truth and also a degree of exaggeration and compulsiveness.

In Richard and Sarah's tale from Chapter 2, subterranean narratives of this kind drove some of their actions and feelings. Young Richard felt unwanted by his family and sought belonging by joining groups. An older Richard felt unappreciated by Sarah and sought belonging by moving away from her. Sarah acted helplessly, resorting to plaintiveness and bewilderment, letting Richard's actions determine her sense of empowerment. She perceived herself to be incapable of joy unless he changed. Both partially hid their emotions, fearing their effects.

At the root of all these stories is an underlying paradigm that only by controlling other people and our external environment can we find a sense of purpose, wellbeing and inner strength. The stories revolve around the need to have others be different than they are, to have the world be different, so that we may be alright. This takes away all our power. We cannot control others. Controlling our environment is possible but requires constant vigilance and will only ever have partial success.

Wanting safety and nurturance from our environment and those around us is a natural impulse, especially from the perspective of a newborn baby, as we all were when we first arrived. Small and helpless, we got our needs met from our primary caregivers. We relied for survival on the actions and the love of our family so of course we embraced their opinions, their life views and their perspectives. There was no need and no capacity for us to pause and consider whether we liked or agreed with those perspectives and values. As the shape of a tree is moulded by the environment in which it begins to grow, our early development is shaped by our family of origin.

But as we mature and develop, we gradually learn to take responsibility for meeting our own needs, for choosing our own views, our values and preferences. We become less dependent on others and on our environment being just so. We discover resources within ourselves. We craft our internal environment and it becomes what gives us our sense of power. We no longer need the people and things around us to be a certain way. When we make our own way, we become free to allow others to be as they are.

This process is what gives us the capacity to go forth and make our life fun and purposeful. We come to know we are complete and we are part of the interconnected web of life. We learn to take responsibility for how we feel, think, express ourselves and act. This is a powerful adult state. The tree becomes robust enough to resist the wind and shape itself.

Yet when the path to maturity is less clear and direct, we may continue, at least in part, to hungrily seek approval and validation from outside ourselves. This can leave us feeling conflicted — resentful of those we depend on for our sense of value and unwilling to believe we can appreciate their love without depending on it. In our efforts to prove our own independence we may learn to ignore the disapproval of others only to inadvertently replace it with the voice of our own inner critic.

Why might the path to maturity be indirect or unclear? Partly because our parents, themselves in the same boat, were not able to be good role models for a self-responsible state. They could not embody the best mix of nurturance and respect to foster our innate sense of wholeness. And also because in popular culture this type of partial maturity is the most frequent model on display. Long after we have left the parental home, we are still surrounded by influences that consolidate disempowering stories.

Richard and Sarah may have had flashes of insight into what patterns of behaviour and thought were preventing them from experiencing more harmony. But they were also bombarded with messages from their friends, relatives and culture that gave support to the old, well-worn and unhelpful patterns. The image of a needy woman with a callous man is one of many common tropes portrayed in novels, movies and real life all over the place. Sarah and Richard could glimpse other possibilities, but those possibilities were hard to believe in among the avalanche of confirmation for that particular overused stereotype.

The answer is not to become a hermit and avoid social contact and cultural influences. Then we would needlessly miss out on the synergy and pleasure of interacting with other humans.

But to best experience that synergy, we need to start from a place of validity.

When we experience ourselves as worthy, valid and complete we are unswayed by irrelevant stereotypes.

From our place of safety and self-acceptance, our interactions with others can become co-creative rather than a co-dependent. Our relationships can augment rather than diminish us, our conversations can inspire us and bring out the best in us, not make us more insecure.

The scripts we run in the background have a significant impact on the success of our relationships and on how we act. They can inform how we interpret our past and what our future holds.

These are all important reasons for paying attention to what stories we tell ourselves. There is another important reason: the stories we tell ourselves also have an impact on our physical bodies and this is what the next chapter is about.

Chapter 5
The Cost Of Stories

Have you ever completely over-reacted to a seemingly small event? Or watched someone else do that? As an observer, it can be perplexing. As the one reacting, it can be distressing.

Paula's neighbour had offered to give her a lift to the local shops to get some supplies, and although Paula didn't really need anything, she thought it would be nice to go together. When she found out her absent-minded neighbour had forgotten and gone without her, Paula felt an intense pang of grief, panic and overwhelm.

Talking with me later, Paula realised her unaccountable distress came from a story: *I've been forgotten. I'm not important. Nobody cares about me, I'm vulnerable, terrified I could get hurt. I'm sad and lonely. I've been abandoned, there is no hope.* Paula's story seemed inappropriate since what happened was trivial, but this story has lain inside Paula for a long time, perhaps since she was very small and she has no clear memory of its origin.

It's easy to conceive of scenarios, real or imagined, where a very young child might feel terrified, believing itself to be abandoned and therefore in mortal danger. Once the association between the situation and the feeling is made, any subsequent experience reminiscent of that situation can trigger the same emotional response, even when the memory of the event is lost.

Paula's story is dormant most of the time, but it comes out of hibernation when something reminds her, however subtly, of what she felt long ago. The *feeling* of being a terrified abandoned child washes over her, no matter how inappropriate it looks to her logical mind. The intense emotions sweep her up, inhibiting her from being her usual cheerful self. Outwardly, Paula got on with her day, forcing herself to act normal. But inwardly those feelings and their physical counterparts, such as the tight knot in her stomach, took many hours to recede.

Paula and I worked together on changing that story. It hardly ever rears its head now and Paula is skilled at switching it right off.

This is good news for Paula as those unpleasant feelings of distress, generated by unhelpful stories, do more than simply feel bad; they impact our physical bodies, our vitality, health and longevity.

Fight or Flight

Inside our physical bodies a million and one messages, instructions, signals and commands are given and received all day long every day we are alive. It's how our brain and our body talk to each other and how different body areas communicate. It happens by molecule, by hormone and by nerve pathway and it happens non-stop. Our bodies are like a finely tuned orchestra with a tireless conductor that plays sweet music 24/7 for our whole life.

Except when the music is not so sweet.

The fight-or-flight system is essential to our survival. Without it we would be indifferent to physical threats and would neither run away from them nor eliminate them. Even if we did think to avoid threats, we would do so ineffectively as there would be no signals leading to the switch in our physiology from baseline to super-efficient high alert. The same system is involved when we make impassioned speeches, dare to climb high mountains and invent flying machines regardless of all the nay-sayers. Life would be dull without the fight-or-flight system!

When your house is on fire or your toddler is stepping out in front of a car, it's important for your entire body's physiology to change, for every organ and tissue to collaborate so you become temporarily super-human, meaning you can run faster, breathe better and react quicker so you can do what you need to do. Adrenaline, noradrenaline and cortisol make this happen, in conjunction with various other processes.

And then it's over. You stop producing the stress hormones, your heart rate and breathing calm down and you return to baseline. It's short, sharp and effective.

During the brief time of the urgent need, your adrenaline, noradrenaline and cortisol signalled your clever body to switch non-urgent functions off, so as to allow maximum efficiency. It switched off things like repairing tissues, digestion, a sense of humour, immune functions and the ability to appreciate fine art. You don't need to compose a sonata or heal a grazed knee when you are faced with a bear in the woods. You do that later, when you're safely away from the bear. That's when those hormones peter out and your clever body switches digestion, tissue repair and art appreciation back on.

Except sometimes the perception of danger doesn't pass so quickly and the danger response keeps on going after the event is over, like a dripping tap.

What we call our difficult emotions are the internal sensations we get when we are in a fight or flight response. There may be no bear. There may be only a forgetful neighbour or a bill to pay. But if a story is operating, we can still feel those sensations that indicate we are under duress. We call those sensations anger, fear, helplessness and all their many variations such as frustration, disappointment, resentment, confusion, resignation and many more.

When you feel scared, angry, helpless or sad, you're experiencing a fight or flight response inside, even though there may be no genuine physical threat to you. You are releasing a burst of adrenaline, noradrenaline and cortisol. This is easy for your finely tuned body to deal with when it lasts a few minutes, as nature intended. You meet the stress, you handle it, then you bounce back to baseline — that's the plan.

Baseline is you calm, collected and confident. Baseline is a constructive and optimistic you. It's where you want to smile, not frown, and it's where birdsong sounds melodic, not irritating. It's where you can't wait to go to the party instead of dreading it and where you have fun writing the presentation instead of thinking it a heinous chore.

If you are running on an unhelpful story that's stuck on replay, your control centre acts like a thermostat gone mad and just keeps on producing stress hormones in response to the script you are running. It perceives you to be in continued danger. That's when the body may experience the physical consequences of telling stories that deplete rather than stories that rejuvenate.

When those stress hormones flow more constantly, like a leaky pipe under the kitchen sink, there are consequences. Under the sink there will be mould and rot. In your physical body it's *catabolism*. That means things breaking down, ageing and wearing out at a faster rate than they can be repaired, because repair functions are on pause.

What breaks down are big things like muscles and bones, and small things like blood vessel walls. Overproducing stress hormones ages you faster than you need to age. It prevents your repair functions from working at their best. It dampens your immunity. It hinders wellness and contributes to illness, poor sleep and poor choices.

When we overproduce cortisol, adrenaline and noradrenaline, we tend to underproduce dopamine, oxytocin, serotonin and endorphins. Some call these our happy hormones. Happy hormones mediate feelings like satisfaction, affection, curiosity and delight. They make us laugh and impel us to create, have fun and contribute.

Whether it's a snake in the shed or an unhelpful story, the result is the same. A prolonged excess of stress hormones combined with a short supply of happy hormones ages you faster and makes you less well.

There will always be life events outside our control that give us a jolt, and that's as it should be. Our threat-defence system handles those, that's what it's designed for. What's meant to happen next is it switches itself off and you merrily get on with life, as you do when the snake is gone from the shed.

Ongoing, overproduction of stress hormones and stressful feelings way after the event is over are less about the event and more about the internal narratives we run about the event. Sometimes, the event is lost to memory and can no longer affect our current reality but the narrative with its associated emotions continue on.

It wasn't missing out on a shopping trip that upset Paula, it was what she made it mean to her. It was the story she was running.

We Can Let Go

No matter how charmed a life someone may lead, it's likely that at some point in time everyone will experience a major life event that really knocks them over. It could be a break up, a bankruptcy or worse. It could be any number of things, as we all react differently to different events. Along with big events, many of us deal with stories like Paula's, where we can't even remember a specific event but we suddenly feel abandoned or betrayed when nothing very much seems to have happened. Sometimes it can feel like these stories are going to go on affecting us forever.

How long does a disturbing and upsetting life event need to go on affecting someone?

Most people who lose a loved one, most people who witness something horrifying, will feel some pretty strong emotions and it would be quite odd if they didn't. But many people go on from there to perpetuate the strong emotions for the rest of their lives because they don't know how to stop replaying the stories of what happened.

It's not uncommon to do this after a divorce or break up. Do you know anyone who has been out of that relationship for decades, yet still tells the story of how they were wronged and continues to define their whole life by what their ex said or did "to" them? In the next chapter you will see how this played out for Richard and Sarah.

Retelling, re-experiencing the story of what happened to us is considered normal and inevitable. It's encouraged by well-meaning others who want to show they care. It's tempting, because there is relief to be had in finding someone who listens and understands. But it can become a habit.

The first few retellings of the story do give relief, they reassure us, they connect us with others, they let us feel normal, they let us come to terms with what happened and they allow us to learn what can be learned from the experience. All these things are helpful.

However it doesn't necessarily go on being helpful forever. There is a danger of getting stuck. Once the reassurance, the connection and the learning have taken place, continuing on with telling the story carries the risk that we stay stuck in it, no longer learning, processing or integrating, but instead defining our life by that story. That's when it can become a lead weight instead of a relief.

When we hear someone telling us for the nth time how badly their ex treated them, it's easy to feel impatient. But replaying the same old story long after it is over is not a stubborn deliberate attempt to be contrary, it's a habit of thought that person has inadvertently fallen into and got stuck in.

They are repeating the event over and over as a mind-movie, telling it to others and to themselves the same way, going over it and consolidating it until it becomes part of the lanscape. It's natural, it's cultural, it's well-intentioned… but it's not helpful.

We don't have to keep doing this.

A story only stays alive because of how often it's repeated, inside our mind or outwardly in our actions and words. This means that if we stop repeating it and tell ourselves better stories instead, we can escape from the cycle of overdosing on stress hormones created by stress-inducing old stories. It means we can allow our hormonal balance to reestablish itself so that happy hormones freely signal joy, levity, trust and abundance. It means we can move on. We can look forward to what's next rather than replay what's past.

It's extremely liberating to understand that you don't have to keep repeating the old cycle!

When fear, frustration, grief or helplessness arise, you can interrupt that fight-or-flight response, you can halt it. This will give you an opportunity to choose a different response and in so doing your body can resume healing and repair processes and your happy hormones can once more flow freely. When you change your stories, you change your body and you enhance your health.

As we move forward, consider the following questions: Would you choose what makes you feel great over what makes you feel horrible? Would you willingly stay, chronically, in feeling sad, sorry, depressed and dissatisfied a minute longer than necessary if you had the option to feel playful, excited, curious and amazed? Would you look at the menu at the restaurant and order the foods you dislike, just because they're on the menu? Or would you order only the yummy ones?

You may think it's not a choice. You may think you have no control over whether you are bathed in stress hormones or bathed in happy hormones. That's okay. We'll take a deeper look at this idea of choice in the next chapter. Until then, don't underestimate yourself.

Chapter 6

You Can Change Your Story

Is changing your story even possible? Isn't it just part of who you are? Aren't stories written in history and therefore we can't change them anyway? And if we have unhelpful beliefs, isn't that what therapy is for?

Stories are indeed narratives that have played a role in shaping who we are and they are made up from our past life experiences. While we can't unlive what we have lived, we can change the way we view what we have lived. Therapy can be one useful aid to changing that view.

A belief, in truth, is just a story you've told yourself enough times you know it by heart — it has become flesh, it's part of who you think you are. It's a view, a tale that has been told, re-told, embellished, edited, and re-told again. It's a full-length mind movie with a soundtrack and special effects. It's a story you have acted out and reimagined so many times that it feels like an essential component of your identity.

You read an account of Richard and Sarah's relationship in Chapter 2. Inside of that story were two unique human beings, each with their own personal perspective, their own individually crafted set of beliefs. They each had their own concept of what was true about them, their situation and each other. This concept, this personal version of their tale, may influence each of them far into the future unless they choose to examine and reframe it. Let us look now at their two versions of the story.

Richard's Perspective

I went out with this woman for a few years, it really didn't work out.

She was just so bloody passive aggressive. It was incredibly annoying. She wouldn't openly say what she wanted; she would just wheedle and whine, slam doors or wear a pitiful look.

When I first met her, she seemed so independent, strong, feisty and self-sufficient. I was a little bit intimidated, maybe a little in awe of her, but obviously it was all a front.

Once the dust settled, she became like this harridan. She was never happy, I couldn't do a thing right and she always looked pissed off. It was like all the fun had gone out of her.

If she was annoyed, which was nearly always, she'd slam doors and throw in covert criticisms non-stop or say sarcastic things about me in front of my family and friends. She never appreciated anything I did so I soon gave up trying.

The weird thing was, she'd done all these amazing things in her life, it was impressive, but when it came down to it, she became this snivelling and complaining person. Obviously it was all just an act and she was never that strong person she pretended to be.

I got really disillusioned. I think women are just weak, they say they're independent but as soon as you spend a bit more time with them they try to be your mother, or they start expecting the world of you and are never satisfied. I'm done with that.

She tried to get my son to believe I was the bad guy of course, they always do that, don't they, bloody manipulative women are. I got my own back, she had no clue what I was up to, left her to stew in her own sourness, served her right, she should have been nicer and more fun to be with.

Sarah's Perspective

Men are bastards. It sounds harsh, but let's face it, it's true. I should know. You can't say I didn't try to find a good one. I had several relationships with very selfish abusive men. They would be all over me at first. I wasn't even that interested, I just went along with it. Then as soon as they thought they had me hooked, they'd show themselves to be the selfish bastard they always were.

They'd become surly, superior, domineering and act like they were the boss. Or they'd cheat, lie, steal and take advantage. Men are users, most men anyway; it's the sad truth. It doesn't matter how nice they seem at first, how many bunches of roses they bring you at first; they just turn into these selfish lazy teenagers without an ounce of self-responsibility.

Take my son's father. Typical. I thought he was going to be different, I thought he was "The One." Stupid me. It all seemed like a fairy tale at first, but he soon showed his true colours. I did my best, I did all the right things. I was kind and understanding. Then when I saw where it was going, I told him straight I wouldn't put up with selfish disrespectful behaviour. I made it clear I wasn't going to stick around and be treated this way.

Did he care? No way. Selfish, didn't give a damn, except about himself. Didn't even help me with the baby. He'd just go off drinking and carousing then sleep all day and leave me to do everything on my own.

So I got rid of him, sent him packing. Good riddance, I say. Men are like that you know. It's just the way it is. Some women put up with their crap but that's just weak. There might be nice decent men out there but I'm not so sure. I've got no time for that sort of thing. Back-stabbers, the lot of them, if you ask me.

Reframing the Story

Did you recognise some of the assumptions and beliefs that lay buried in Richard's and Sarah's accounts of their relationship? Beliefs and assumptions can be hard to uncover, they seem like part of the furniture. But uncovering them can be worthwhile as the stories and beliefs we hold, often only partly in our awareness, are a large element of what guides the direction of our life.

If those stories and beliefs contain messages that we must endure physical or emotional discomfort, that our unhappiness is the fault of others, that we're the bad guys or that we do everything right and are the victim of bad guys, then we may needlessly deprive ourselves of the happiness and fulfilment we would otherwise experience.

Reframing our beliefs, composing new stories to replace old ones can be helpful actions. This means taking those beliefs from the realm of unquestioned rules from the past and moulding them into different beliefs. These new beliefs act as guidelines for living a life we choose for ourselves, rather than a life blindly directed by outdated stories.

"I have to do everything on my own" can become "I didn't ask for help because I was expecting others to read my mind, but I'm getting better at expressing myself more clearly." "All men are bastards" can become "Well, that relationship didn't work so well, but I learned a lot from it and there's probably someone out there that's a much better match for me." "I'm the bad guy" can become "I was acting from false beliefs and didn't like the results, so I'm glad I noticed that and can now see more clearly how I want to act going forward."

By rewording the stories we live by, we can be a much more conscious director of our own life path.

Emotions As Guidance

Sometimes, though, it can be difficult to identify the beliefs we might want to change. In considering which beliefs are helpful and which are less so, examining our emotions can provide clarification.

When you think about your life experience, do you prefer to feel happy or sad? Frustrated or satisfied? Inspired or discouraged? Do you prefer to experience a sense of success or a sense of failure? For most of us, the answers will be obvious. Behind each of these emotions is a well-practised thought which has become a belief. If you are experiencing some frustration or disappointment, you can ask yourself what the belief is that leads to those feelings.

Many years ago in Sydney on the morning of my son's 5th birthday party I felt those very things, frustrated and disappointed. My friend who was bringing the birthday cake blithely arrived 3 hours late, totally missing the appointed birthday cake moment I had carefully planned.

The narrative leading to my frustration was: "I'm embarrassed some kids had to leave without cake or seeing the candles blown out, the other mothers will think I'm terrible. This unexpected situation demands that I allocate blame and experience anger. My happiness and satisfaction depend on others acting as I expect them to. What I have learned today is that my friend doesn't care about me and can't be trusted or relied on. I shall note that down in my mental ledger for posterity."

This narrative may seem logical and reasonable, but it is disempowering. A more empowering story would be: "Sometimes things go to plan and sometimes they don't, I'm capable of finding satisfaction regardless. Because of the missing cake I had to think creatively and exercise my serenity muscles so I'm better equipped for the next time things don't go as expected. This experience has confirmed to me that I do enjoy when things go to plan so next time I will make different arrangements for the cake."

Your emotions can be an excellent prompt for you to examine the thoughts behind those emotions and the beliefs and stories behind the thoughts.

In this case, my frustration and disappointment showed me there was something to be examined. I did not do it immediately! I needed to experience my frustration and disappointment first, but over time, with some calm and objectivity, I did gradually change my thoughts and beliefs about that incident. It now only makes me chuckle affectionately at both my friend and myself, in the knowledge that I can love her just as much even while I choose other means of getting cakes to arrive on time.

Had I left my belief unchallenged, I might have used the incident as "proof" for my story. Concluding that my story was correct, holding myself apart from viewing it any other way, I could have gone on experiencing similar incidents, each one adding to the burden of "evidence" that people can't be trusted. It's not a particularly fun or light-hearted way to feel. If your preference is for more enjoyable emotions, you can achieve that through reframing a story.

Checking in with your emotions and asking what thoughts and beliefs underlie them is an effective way to sort and sift and decide which beliefs to keep. If a belief works for you, makes your life more beautiful, makes you happy, then it's worth keeping. If a belief makes you mad, sad or bad, why entertain it and give it airtime? Why go to a horror movie if you hate being scared? Why watch a tragic love story if you're already feeling blue?

This doesn't only apply to your own stories. We want to show we care by listening to other people's sad stories, but that may not be the best way to care. Listening to your friend complaining endlessly about their intractable elderly father when you're already overwhelmed by your own intractable elderly father only makes both of you feel more overwhelmed.

You don't have to tell (or listen to) stories of woe or helplessness, or stories of anger and wrongdoing if those stories cause you grief. As we saw in the last chapter, sharing our difficult stories can bring support and solidarity but we need to then move on or we risk amplifying our distress. If a story isn't making you feel good, it may be time to change it.

The Greater Good

However sometimes difficult emotions are the natural result of something we have chosen to do. There are times when we will embrace pain and discomfort for the sake of a greater aim. Childbirth, studying for an exam or staying all night at someone's bedside are examples of this. So are climbing Mount Everest or fasting.

Enduring uncomfortable emotions and sensations for a specific reason, with a specific intention, is a part of life. However, enduring those things when there is no benefit, when they are simply a habit of thought we are unaware we can cease, isn't productive.

As you follow your chosen path and pursue your goals, there will be moments of boredom, exhaustion and despair. This is the hero's journey. Obstacles must be traversed to achieve our cherished aims. It's a natural element of personal growth. If you are experiencing pain or distress, you can learn to distinguish whether you're choosing this path because you're on your way to an imporant goal or because you're stuck in an old story that isn't leading anywhere in particular.

In my youth I gladly spent many uncomfortable nights sleeping on airport benches, hours waiting for buses or queuing for cash, fearful moments when I wandered into the wrong side of town and periods of boredom from missed trains and overlong castle tours. All of these I endured cheerfully for the greater aim (at least to me) of experiencing an exotic destination and witnessing weird wonderful things. It was more than worth it.

Later in life I accidentally fell into a different travel story, where on planning a trip I would approach the process with dread, predicting broken websites, false information, bad-tempered airline staff and overpriced accommodation. I uncovered an absurd narrative I was running in the background, portraying me as the victim of a conspiracy that singled me out for every kind of travel obstacle, as if I had been cursed. My mind created this silly story without my really noticing, in response to somewhat paranoid thoughts following a series of stressful travel mishaps. There was no greater aim and no upside. Once I realised what I was doing it was easy to let it go. My travel plans have returned to being simple and smooth!

Since we can choose the stories we tell and thus the stories that play out for us, let us choose the stories that aid us in achieving our goals and desires, rather than those that simply hamper us without a benefit.

In the next chapter, we'll look at one of the most accepted but unhelpful stories that can greatly affect how joyfully you live your life.

Chapter 7
That Age-Old Story

Have you ever thought somewhat despondently to yourself that you were getting old? If so, how old were you when that thought first occurred to you?

The topic first appeared to me as I turned 10. An adult, wishing perhaps to impress with their cleverness and wisdom, pointed out to me that I would never again have only 1 digit to my age. This was not the most enlightening piece of information I ever received from an adult.

The topic appeared again two decades later as my 30-year-old housemate told me that no, he would not act on his wish to learn to play the piano, because he was too old for that. Fortunately, the extreme absurdity of that remark led me to reconsider my opinion on ageing and form a much better one than the first experience had given me.

There is a story about ageing, about getting old. It's about how terrible it is, how sad and unfortunate it is. It's about how it always and inevitably comes with major suffering, an inability to use the remote control, painful slowness of thought and action, chronic disease and probably cancer too.

You may think: well yes, that's what happens. We gradually lose our hearing, our eyesight and our mental marbles. Our joints go stiff and things hurt, and before you know it your driving licence has been taken from you and you're drooling in the corner with a kind but hurried nurse feeding you tasteless goop.

Or you can think: wait a minute. My aunt Mavis worked on the farm til she was 96 and did all the jobs and marched across the field to have words with the bull and dropped dead one day with a smile on her face. You can think: wait a minute, what about Joan McDonald who began bodybuilding for the first time at 71 and is now, at 82, medication-free, strong as an ox and all over Instagram? You may remember your trip across Asia or Africa where you saw grey-haired great-grandparents comfortably squatting to wait for a bus or easily carrying a massive load. You may have read the book *Born to Run* where you learned that a 60-year-old ultramarathon runner is, on average, only 5% slower than a 20-year-old ultramarathon runner.

There are two ways to age. There is the one portrayed in the commonly-told story. The other way of ageing is that taken by aunt Mavis, Joan McDonald and the octogenarians in parts of the world where a different story is told. Which of the two becomes your life story is rarely down to an act of God, bad luck or genetics. It can be those things, but rarely. Mostly it's down to swallowing the lie that it's down to bad luck, genetics and acts of God. It's a story. Not a particularly helpful one.

I'm Old

Recently I reconnected with a friend on the phone, after two decades. He's 11 years younger than me. "I'm old", he said. He said it twice during our conversation, about nothing in particular. I hadn't asked him. It took me by surprise. Actually, it shocked me.

Why did he say that? Why was it so much on his mind that he mentioned it twice when the conversation had no relation to age? I didn't know how to respond. It made me realise, with a flush of gratitude, that (perhaps thanks to my earlier non-piano-learning friend), I don't identify as old. The story I was told when I was 10 has been replaced with a different one.

I do know when I was born, I am aware of how many years ago that was, but that number is rarely of any particular relevance or interest. It doesn't feature in my conversations unless the topic specifically requires it. This incident did remind me of an endearing habit my grandmother, Doris, acquired once she showed a few early signs of dementia. When at a restaurant and someone arrived to take our order, she would make sure to inform them: "I'm 96, you know!"

Of course time passes and our bodies become less vital and less mobile. But the difference in physical capacity between a 25-year-old and a 95-year-old does not, simply by virtue of age, have to be a vast chasm. It can be relatively small. All over the globe and in every era of history there are examples of this. *Those* people's stories rarely appear in mainstream media, which instead bombards us with messages of illness, medication, walking sticks, hearing aids, dependency and decrepitude. It's no wonder we get the impression that is our unavoidable fate.

Environmental, lifestyle and dietary factors have an obvious effect on our physical health, but too often, we minimise the impact our beliefs have on health and aging. You can choose to live your life according to stories that uplift, rejuvenate and enliven you. When you do that, you will feel and act more youthfully, which in turn leads you to gravitate naturally towards the best lifestyle and dietary factors for your wellbeing.

I read that in 1979, psychologist Ellen Langer took eight men in their 70s to a monastery in New Hampshire and left them there for 5 days with instructions to feel, think, speak and behave as if it were 1959, with decor, music and movies to match. They came out 5 days later with taller sitting posture, better cognition and improved health. This may not constitute proof of anything but it's impressive whichever way you look at it. Proof or no proof, don't we all intuitively know that if you treat people as if they are inept, slow-witted and defective that's going to have an effect?

What Season Are You In?

Our culture tells us we can expect to live to be about 80, so our seasons of life might follow this framework: spring is age 1-20, summer is age 20-40, autumn is age 40-60 and winter is age 60-80. And then you die.

By this measure, I'm at the start of winter.

What if you take your frame of reference to be 100 years? Now spring is 1-25, summer is 25-50, autumn is 50-75 and winter is 75-100. I'm already feeling warmer. Now I'm only in mid-autumn.

I've taken it a step further. I'm using a 120-year frame! Spring is 1-30, summer is 30-60, autumn is 60-90 and winter is 90-120. I'm still in autumn, but now I'm right at the very beginning of autumn. I feel positively adolescent!

But studies prove our life expectancy is about 80, so you can't expect to live to be 120!

At the time of writing, life expectancy for both sexes combined is published at 73 across the globe, and 80-85 for more prosperous countries.

This figure is the average life expectancy at birth. Average. At birth. If 100 babies are born on the same day in Australia, some will die at birth, some at age 3, some at 15, some at 60 and some at 104 and a half. When you average this out, you get 85.

It does not mean that Australians can expect to drop dead at exactly the age of 85. It does not mean that death cannot come just as easily for a 3-year-old as for a 93-year-old. It does not mean that from the day of your 85th birthday you are living on borrowed time. At any age you can be hit by a bus. At any age you can get cancer or a serious illness. At any age you still have an unknown number of productive years left and at any age you can learn the piano.

Why would you use an average to predict what will happen to you who are a one-of-a kind individual? That would be like never starting a business because someone told you 95% of businesses fail. It would be like never running because it takes you longer than the average 10 minutes to run a mile.

Can you still enjoy running? Are there factors that make some businesses fail and others succeed, including factors you can control? Is a business failure always a bad thing? What if the lessons learned from a few business failures lead you to heights undreamed of? What if running, albeit a little slower than Usain Bolt, gives you pleasure and you don't give a hoot about your speed?

You don't need to let your enjoyment of life from birth until death be marred by what a statistician found when he or she pooled together a bunch of semi-reliable data points about longevity across the globe and concluded something about you.

You can choose how you tell the story of how you want your life to unfold.

No law compels you to tell it the way it is for many people and the way it is portrayed in the media. You don't know what's coming. Predicting disaster doesn't avert disaster and it can frighten you without bringing any advantage.

Every day is a new day where you decide how you're going to feel about life. Every day you can refine and polish the story of you, as you continue to live another day and then another.

Can you really unlearn old stories and learn new ones? That's what the next chapter is all about.

Chapter 8
You Have What it Takes

You may not be convinced it's possible to change your stories. It may seem too hard. It may seem like it's too late. It may seem like a silly, implausible idea.

Yet your nervous system and your brain are highly malleable and therefore capable of learning and unlearning things. That's what people are talking about when they use the term neuroplasticity.

Neuroplasticity is just a fancy word to describe the capacity we all have for learning to think, feel, function and behave in new ways. It's our ability to put into practice new ways of being, through a gradual process of adaptation and skills acquision.

When you learn a skill, you create a pathway in your nervous system, a series of neurons connecting with other neurons in just the right order to create the desired action. You do this your whole life. As you have probably observed, old dogs can learn new tricks. Sometimes it takes old dogs a little bit longer, but no dog is past learning a new trick or two. If you are an old dog, this should give you some satisfaction.

Not only can you learn new skills, you can unlearn old skills and replace them with better ones. If you learned to hold your tennis racket inefficiently and then you gradually refined a more effective grip and thus improved your tennis, this is what you did. You demonstrated neuroplasticity. Your neuronal pathways rearranged themselves in a way that works better for you in terms of playing tennis. Over the next few weeks or months, the new neuronal pathways became gradually smoother, more robust and reliable. They became your new baseline.

A pathway made up of connected neurons leading to new skills is similar to a well-worn path through the forest. While people walk that well-worn path, it stays there, reliable and known. But if people start going through the forest a different way, the old path starts to get overgrown. The grass grows back, bushes obscure it, branches fall across it. The old path looks less and less appealing, it becomes harder to see and it starts to disappear. The new path becomes the well-worn, reliable and known way through the forest. After a time you barely remember there even was another path.

You can unlearn the stories you keep telling yourself by learning different stories. You can replace the pathway in your mind that says "I'm not good enough" with a pathway in your mind that truthfully says "I'm doing great."

Because when you tell stories that say you're doing great, you do actually start doing great. Not always instantaneously, but a lot quicker than most people realise.

In the beginning it takes some conscious effort. But once you learn a skill, after a time it becomes automatic. You become unconsciously competent. Remember when you couldn't drive a car? It took some weeks or months (or years). One step at a time, one concept after another, each micro-skill building on the last. Most likely it wasn't a linear process. There were times you learned something which you then forgot and had to learn again. It's likely you did things jerkily, stiffly and awkwardly at first. But over time you smoothed out your actions. You got frustrated some days and thought you'd never learn and other days you had big leaps forward. That's how learning goes.

As you practised, you consolidated your new skill. Now, you could drive a car without a hiccup even if you went decades without even seeing one. Assuming cars haven't changed too much.

The Backwards Brain Bicycle

Let's look at an example of that process from a more novel perspective.

Destin Sandlin is a man who invented, just for fun, a bicycle with the handlebars adjusted so that when you turn them to the left the bike goes right and vice versa. He toured universities demonstrating his bike and all the volunteers who tried to ride it fell off immediately. Destin himself of course, trained and trained until he could ride it. So did his young son, who apparently took only two weeks to succeed. After Destin had mastered his own bike, he tried to ride a normal bike. I saw an amusing video of him on YouTube attempting this and falling off repeatedly.

Destin had replaced his long-standing pathways for riding a normal bike with the new pathway for riding the reverse handlebar bike. Like Destin did with his bike, you can replace your habit of thinking negatively with habits of thinking positively, if you so choose. Because thinking a certain way is a skill, just like riding a bike is a skill, even though one skill is more outwardly visible than the other.

In Destin's case, he did want to go back to riding a regular bike, so he practised again until he could. It took him less than an hour, since that long-standing skill was still fresh and the new one was only brand new. I don't know how the story ends, perhaps Destin has two sets of bikes in his shed, or perhaps he sticks to the one he prefers.

There's almost no limit to our ability to build skills on top of each other. An actor switches easily between various accents and between characters. You yourself may switch easily from tennis to ping pong or squash. As a child it was normal for me to switch between English, French and Portuguese at the dinner table, I didn't know any different. Children of musicians may play multiple instruments before they can read.

Anyone is capable of switching between accents, racket games and languages. It may be effortless if we are born into a certain environment, or it may occur through consciously seeking to learn. Either way, neuroplasticity ensures success because it's innately available to all of us. Equally, anyone can learn to switch up the roles or characters they act out and the stories they live by. This is because everyone has a nervous system which is the only piece of equipment you need.

If something doesn't come easy straight away, it doesn't mean you can't learn and should give it up as impossible. The first time you went to a salsa class you felt like you had two left feet and were never going to be able to dance, and now look at you! I'll trust you to replace "salsa" with a word of your choice that makes sense for you.

Some skills you acquired easily and some didn't work out for you. There will be some skills you tried to learn that you gave up on. It's not because you are incapable of learning those skills!

There isn't much you are incapable of. If you gave up, it could be that you simply weren't interested and had better things to do. Or it could be that you approached the learning with a story that said: *I can't. I don't believe it. It's not going to work for me.*

These are the only things that prevent learning new skills: lack of desire for, or interest in, that particular skill, or a false narrative that blocks our progress.

If changing your stories Is of no interest to you, there's no reason you should do it, go spend your time on something you are interested in.

If changing your stories *is* of interest to you, the only thing in your way is a story. That's great news! It means you have something straight away to start working with.

Ninja Not Necessary

There is a difference between *mastery* and competence. *Mastery* means you are at a level where doing the new skill is as natural as breathing. *Competence* means you are at the level where you can do it well enough for your purposes. There are different levels of competence, just as there are different belts in martial arts.

There is no need to become a ninja or black belt. Even a stumbling, beginner level of skill in telling better stories about your life will bring many rewards. These will come in the form of more fulfilment, peace and pleasure. They will also come as greater harmony in your hormonal balance and biochemistry, benefiting your physical self.

What matters is that you are willing to practice your new skill over a period of time. The time it takes to replace old stories will depend on several factors: your level of commitment and consistency, the stubbornness of your stories and the attitudes you bring to the idea of change. A realistic time frame for creating new thought habits could be anything from a few weeks to a couple of years.

Everything we learn can be unlearned and replaced. Every story and belief can be edited or re-written. Just as an actor can learn a character inside out and then drop it so they can play another part or be themselves off camera, we too can drop a story and choose another.

The idea that we can't change is just another replaceable story. If you're not so sure about that, the next 3 chapters may give you more trust in your abilities.

62   **Tell Yourself Better Stories** Doris Hasslocher

Chapter 9
But I'm Limited

It's natural when trying on a new idea, like the idea of changing your internal narratives, to experience resistance, objections and doubts.

Misgivings may arise as thoughts: *this doesn't work and isn't true;* or *this is all very nice but it can't work for me;* or *this may have validity but it can't work in the way being presented and I don't trust the person presenting it.* Or misgivings may appear as emotions such as overwhelm, helplessness, irritation, disdain, sorrow or self-pity.

It's valuable to note this. Objections and doubts are there to protect us from harm, so we should listen to them, not dismiss them. It's just that sometimes our objections and doubts are coming from one of our stories and could be standing in the way of our goals and desires.

The art of discerning if a feeling of reluctance should be believed and acted on or if that feeling of reluctance would be best reframed is one you refine naturally as you practice it.

We will explore possible sources of doubt in this and the next few chapters and you will feel better equipped to make that distinction, which only you can make.

Real and Perceived Limitations

We all have certain limitations. We can't fly or jump over the top of a building. We can't see through mountains or pass through walls. We can't turn into a deer and we can't fall from an aeroplane at 30,000 feet and survive. We can't run as fast as a horse or climb as well as a monkey. Our body cannot use aspartame as a nutrient.

Along with these very real limitations, many of us have a collection of perceived limitations. I'm no good at learning languages. I have a hot temper. I don't understand tech. I'm not attractive and never will be because my nose is too big and my boobs are too small. I will always be poor because I come from a poor family. Life is hard, painful and short. I'm afraid of heights.

In the book *Psychocybernetics*, author Maxwell Maltz refers to a diagram of two boxes. The outer box represents our real limitations. Inside that box there is another box, much smaller, representing our perceived limitations. We create that one with our beliefs. The inner box can be changed, expanded or perhaps even removed altogether, whereas the outer box can't (unless you know something I don't).

Many of us are quite certain our limitations are real. "But I really am bad at languages! I've tried repeatedly and always failed. I really am unattractive, it's just a fact. I've been bad with money my whole life, it's a real limitation, I have proof."

These perceptions *are* real to us. Why are they real? Because we have been seeing ourselves that way, saying those things to ourselves for so long those beliefs have become entrenched. That doesn't mean it has to remain true forever. For every perception you have, there is an option to perceive the same situation in the exact opposite way.

Rocks and Wrinkles

Isn't it interesting that two people can see the same thing in the mirror, for example a bigger-than-average nose, and have totally different thoughts and feelings on what that means? One person may admire their nose and see it as strong, interesting and characterful. Another could see in their mirror a very similar nose and decide it's ugly, grotesque and offensive to others. Each person believes in their truth just as much as the other.

For many years I hated seeing my wrinkles in the mirror. The first time this happened I was in my early 30s and barely had any. Things didn't improve as time passed. I accepted my fate as gracefully as I could, but the fact remained: my wrinkles were there in the mirror and they made me ugly, there was no argument.

Then one day as I walked on a beautiful beach admiring interesting-looking rocks covered in criss-crossing meandering lines, I suddenly saw that these lines were like my wrinkles. And the lines on the rocks were not ugly, they were beautiful. The lines on the rocks told the rocks' story, they told of the eons passed on this beach, the rains, the waves and the winds which shaped those rocks. I like to think it told of the things they had seen, the adventures they had had.

I went back to the mirror and applied that framework to my face. My wrinkles were telling my story, every line made of the events, joys and sorrows of a life well lived.

For a while I made a conscious effort to speak to myself positively about my wrinkles, to individually thank and celebrate them. I was swapping out an old story that didn't serve me for a new one that does.

I won't say I don't ever revert back to my old story, but it's no longer my default setting when I see myself. It only pops up if I'm temporarily feeling a bit despondent, which is pretty rare these days. Most of the time I smile at them, like old friends.

Being Right

Why do we want so much to hang on to our perceived limitations, even when we know they aren't helping? One explanation is by way of the grandly named Reticular Activating System found in your brain. Its various functions include drawing attention to facts and evidence that validate what you perceive to be true. It's like a heat-seeking missile, but instead of seeking heat, it's seeking to confirm you're right, about all the things you know and think you know.

This is helpful when we're young, because it's reassuring to know the world around us is a reliable place. It would be unsettling at a tender age to entertain doubts about all the things we are learning from our family.

We take what our parents say, do, think and feel at face value, and our trusty RAS supports us by showing us lots of proof that what we're learning is useful and correct. Without it, young children would feel they were on shaky ground, making them anxious and inhibiting their learning.

So the Reticular Activating System does an important job and does it well. It's your trusty fact checker — except it's not really that trusty. It has a huge bias: it wants you to be right. Its research is not objective and it disregards evidence that might point to a mistaken belief. It wants at all costs to bolster and reassure you, so as to help you feel safe in the world. This works great when most of the elements of your evolving worldview are helpful ones.

What about when they're not?

Our view of ourselves and the world arose gradually and subliminally as we matured and continues to evolve our whole life. Our image of ourself and of how things work is part of us and most of us don't question it any more than we question the fact that we breathe air, drink water and need to go to the toilet. That world view includes what you perceive to be your limitations and you don't question those either.

You may never have wondered whether your ability to sing is in fact merely undeveloped, rather than non-existent. You may never have considered that a facial blemish could be seen as an asset. You may be unaware that your troubles with technology are not structural but merely a story.

Depending on what became normal for you as you grew up, you may continue to act on the dictum that big boys don't cry and good girls dress demurely. You may see it as inescapable law that you belong to X political party, Y religion or Z social sphere. Perhaps you never considered whether all children are best served by attending school and whether it really is necessary to eat three meals a day at similar times and consume cereals every morning.

This effect extends further than just how we see ourselves, it's also in our expectations and our actions. You may fully expect water to flow freely into your kitchen sink at a touch of your hand, your toilet to flush and your garbage to be picked up every Wednesday without your having to do anything to make it happen. You may automatically take a bottle of wine when invited for dinner, recycle your plastics, eat with a knife and fork. These are the things we don't examine because they are have become normal to us.

For every one of these examples, there are people you haven't met, somewhere on this beautiful planet, whose normal is entirely different. Their normal could potentially be shocking and barely believable to you, just as your normal might be to them.

If you have ever moved from Australia to El Salvador as I did in 2022, you may have been equally surprised to discover that washing dishes by filling the sink with hot soapy water was not the only path to clean dishes. Across the continent of Latin America people have been happily using cold running water and a compressed cake of powdered soap and achieving perfectly satisfactory results. There are no absolutes when it comes to what's "normal."

Changing Your Wardrobe

Becoming an adult includes conducting an audit of what we consider normal so we can make conscious choices about which elements of our normal to keep and which to discard. It's not unlike going through your wardrobe now and then and getting rid of the things you don't want to wear any more. You can do the same with your perceived limitations.

We constantly have new experiences. They show us which of our perceived limitations no longer need constrain us and which of our borrowed opinions we no longer agree with. This frees us.

We are continually gaining new information and new frames of reference, it's the natural process of growth and adaptability and a path to a better and better life. Holding on to outdated perceptions, behaviours and belief patterns only keeps us in a cage.

Everyone can develop the capacity to be more adaptable, to more freely allow for a world view which evolves in the face of new data.

When you do encounter new data that makes you question your current world view, the first step is becoming aware of it on an intellectual level. This is only the start. Your loyal RAS won't let you get away so easily, its job is to confirm you've been correct all this time. It wants you to hang on to what you've considered normal, at least until your new world view has a bit more to back it up. If you have ever tried to give up smoking, it probably didn't happen on the very first day you intellectually decided you didn't want to smoke.

You can see this play out in many ways. You may hear someone profess to "live and let live" while battling daily to mould their mother, child or spouse into someone else they think would be better than the original. Others may complain bitterly about some awful behaviour only to perform that same behaviour in a different context without making the connection.

Knowing something mentally is only scratching the surface. For real change we need to go a layer deeper.

When we truly have changed our world view, when we have successfully given up smoking, when we have ceased to try to change our parent, child or friend, it's because we've reached that deeper layer. A new world view has opened to us, a different belief has become our foundation.

How long this takes depends on how strongly we hold the former belief and on the focus and intention we place on modifying it. When we have reached that deeper layer of change, we see ourselves differently. We are a non-smoker, an acceptor of that person exactly as they are and now our actions efforlessly flow from this new image of ourselves and our world.

When I first had the thought about wrinkles and rocks, I didn't instantly switch into loving my wrinkles. But I did instantly realise it was a good idea to think that way. And so I nurtured that idea patiently over the next many months. Gradually it became my new frame of reference and the old frame fell away, obsolete.

Perceived limitations come in many forms besides believing we can't sing or are unattractive and we can change them via the same process. But what about our emotional habits? Can we change those too?

Many people believe that emotions just happen, that they arrive in us because of an external event. From this it follows logically that the only way to control our emotions is to control external events. This includes controlling and influencing other people. This can be an overwhelming and exhausting prospect!

But the idea that our emotions are not under our volitional control is just another story that may not necessarily serve us.

How do you feel when you consider that your feelings are caused by outside forces? How do you feel if you now contemplate the idea that you do have some control and influence over your feelings? Which belief feels better to you? Which one gives you a sense of power? Which one do you **choose** to believe in?

You can change your emotional habits the same way you change any other perceived limitation — by changing your stories and the beliefs that underlie your stories. It may be slower and more involved than changing your wardrobe, but not by as much as you may think. It does require the new stories to be told, re-told, refined and repeated over a period of time. It won't be instant. But it is inevitable, if you choose to commit to it.

What you perceive and what you believe about yourself has a profound impact on your wellbeing, your longevity, your success, your ability to support others and your imprint on this world.

But what if my unhelpful story is true? Let's talk about that next.

Chapter 10
But It's True

Letting go of outdated stories can be challenging because they contain truth, they contain facts and events that really happened.

It's true I can't pay my bills this month. It's true my partner left me. It's true the tradesman was overcharging me. It's true my parents were alcoholics. It's true there's a war in that country and people are dying. It's true there are toxins in the rivers and fish are being poisoned, I've seen the dead fish. It's true there are murderers and despots abusing power, it's in the news and the history books.

While circumstances may be verifiably true, reality is more complex. Later, you may discover it was not as simple as you thought, there was another side to the story, or the information provided was incomplete, mistaken, or even a pack of lies. But a lot of it really is true, really can be demonstrated to be factual, with photos, records and proof.

What is Helpful?

There are some questions about stories that may be more important than merely their accuracy.

As I have alluded to throughout this book, one of those questions is whether it is helpful to dwell on the bills, the wars or the poisoned fish.

Is it helpful to me or to the world at large, if I, from way over here in a different place, torture myself with worry and impotent rage about those things? Does worrying make me a better person or relieve others of the suffering I imagine they feel? Is anything achieved when I focus my distress on something way over there that I can't really influence?

You may be thinking that if you think about it enough you will think of a way to remedy, to right the wrongs and rectify the injustices. With all that thinking, maybe you will. That would be wonderful, because building better systems and finding a path through difficulty may well bring more harmony into the world.

But if you want to find that solution, justice, or remedy, what will give you better results? Will you come up with a solution more easily when in a state of guilt, anger and despair or in a state of courage, creativity, and clear thinking?

I once watched helplessly as two people I was working with on making adobe bricks in Brazil argued for over two hours about whether the reason the adobe bricks cracked overnight was down to not adding enough water or using the incorrect ratio of sand with the clay. No forward progress was made, the need to be right was too strong. The mistaken belief that any benefit could come from repeatedly asserting a perceived truth led to absolutely nothing being achieved. For two hours the dialogue consisted of variations on: it's the water, no it's the sand, no it's the water, no it's the sand.

We could have asked someone more experienced in the village. We could have planned an experiment to test each hypothesis. We could have paused for a cup of tea, we could have laughed about it while hurling bricks at the ground. We could have said a prayer to the adobe gods or done an adobe dance or built a doll's house from broken bricks. All of those things would have been more helpful than what we actually did — them arguing heatedly, me watching in mounting frustration.

But what they were saying was *true* to them. One of them was certain it was the water while the other was certain it was the sand and they were on a mission to have their truth be the winner. Where did their devotion to truth get them? It got them stuck in a cycle of butting heads for more than two hours. Two hours they could have spent going for a walk, playing backgammon or writing that thank you letter to their uncle.

When we ask ourselves the question "Is this true?" our mind goes straight to logic and to weighing up evidence on either side. We may become combative, defending the evidence we think we have.

But we don't have all the evidence, and we can't possibly ever have it all. We do not know every factor that contributed to the war and we do not know what our teenager was thinking when they left the kitchen in a mess. Nobody has all the facts and even if they did, the facts are open to interpretation.

When I was in Brazil, none of us knew much about adobe bricks, but even if we had all been experts we would have had different opinions. Just ask a group of coffee experts what makes the perfect cup of coffee, then take cover.

No matter how diligently we investigate, or rely on someone else's diligent investigation, there will always be unknowns, errors, intangibles and inexplicables. There will always be more than one possible answer. Relying only on evidence is risky and prone to error. It can lead us to feel even more ill-equipped to make a choice on what to believe and how to act. Consulting experts can lead to clarity or, just as easily, augment our confusion.

Focusing only on facts and expert opinions takes us away from the bigger picture, which could be to realise we can't solve this right now or it's not ours to solve or we have better things to do with our time than worry about whether something is true or not.

Rather than asking if something is true, what if we we were to ask instead "What would be helpful here?"

With that question, our mind will bypass our intellect's insistence on minutely examining an impossibly long list of known or supposed facts. When we ask what is helpful, our mind goes to the enormous and barely conscious repository of past experience, instinct, values, knowledge and memories we hold. Here it hones in on the most expedient, simple and all-round satisfactory response to whatever situation we are facing.

This aspect of us is far more powerful and efficient than we give it credit for. You may call it your right brain, your creative mind or your subconscious. You may call it instinct, a higher self, the infinite field of possibilities or you can call it Dave if you like.

Whatever you choose to call it, with great skill it will assess your current situation, your current likes and dislikes, your current understanding and it will suggest to you a course of action that fits with all relevant factors as best as possible.

It can take a little practice to allow that part of ourselves to act, to learn to trust it, instead of reverting to what school taught us to do: look at the facts, all the facts, nothing but the facts.

We can awaken this power by asking better questions. Asking what is true may be less effective than asking what is helpful. I know it's not what our university lecturers told us to do, or all those books about decision-making, but how does it feel, when you try it on?

Now if the question at hand is about whether you can afford the house, or whether to have that operation, then, depending on your level of understanding, it may well be more appropriate to rely more heavily on facts, logic and experts. But even then, it would be wise to let your instinctual self in on the decision as well.

And when it comes to your teenager's kitchen skills, what to think about the war or the looming crisis and what to do about the cracked bricks, all the facts are not going to be available or reliable. That's when it would be way more helpful to consider what's helpful.

Evidence and facts are very handy and lots of fun, but let them be an adjunct to your growing trust in yourself, not the one and only tool you use.

Where to Invest Your Resources

Another question to consider, ahead of whether something is true or not, is whether you actually can do anything or if it's your responsibility to do something. If there's an ill-defined crisis far away, are you physically, emotionally or financially equipped to help or are your resources better spent on those near you or indeed on yourself?

Being consumed by a desire to remedy or prevent something you cannot understand or physically affect takes your focus away from spending time and energy nearer to home where you can have more impact.

It's completely natural to care about other people's suffering but this can be taken too far. Caring does not need to take our focus away from our own lives.

Guilt-inducing messages, implying we must sacrifice ourselves for others, are commonplace. They're on the news, in soap operas and in novels, they're embedded in commercials and customs. We are frequently enjoined to believe that the only way to be a worthy human is to deny our own needs, and even our own family's needs, in order to meet the needs of someone needier still.

Altruism is innate to us and heroic acts, such as diving into a lake to save someone, are common across cultures. The book *Humankind* by Rutger Bregman is replete with examples of such acts and does a great job of showing humanity in a much better lightr than mainstream media usually does.

But acts of altruism needn't become sacrificial acts, needn't lead us to a state of permanent guilt and inadequacy just because we can't save everyone from everything. We may hear and know about all sorts of suffering occurring across the globe, but our natural sense of caring need not extend to a vain desire to aid or prevent every instance of suffering.

A constant burden of guilt about what we think we should be doing and are not doing only leaves us feeling powerless. That isn't helpful to anyone and because feeling that way is exhausting it could make us less likely to be altruistic if the opportunity arises.

My dear friend Hannah felt deeply guilty for not going to a country she knew to be at war, for not leaving her young sons and her husband in order to go physically there. She yearned to help the people she could see nightly on the news in their suffering. It was palpable to her because in the past she had done humanitarian work in countries ravaged by natural disasters and war. It was real to her, she knew in a practical sense how to help, how to bring order and comfort, she'd done it before.

She lay awake wishing she could go and believing she was selfish for not going. In that state, she was neither here nor there. She was with her family, but not really, because her guilt kept her distracted. Her desire to help people in that country was impotent, she was in limbo.

A part of Hannah could not fully commit to the choice she had made of staying with her family and so she was unable to be the positive influence in their lives that she normally was. She beat herself up daily, criticising her choice to stay.

Whether a difficult situation is far away or right next door, this same conflict may arise. The truth is no usefulness can come from having conflicting desires, from wanting to help when we are not able to help or helping is not our work.

Worry, pity and concern obstruct the ability to think creatively. This means we miss out and our loved ones miss out. It also means we're too busy feeling powerless to have any good ideas that actually might help someone.

Hannah found peace once she understood her decision to stay with her family was the most helpful one she could make.

Must It Be True To Be Valid?

The other side of this coin is that what is most helpful need not always be true! This can be as simple as successfully keeping up morale by choosing to believe help is on the way even when we have no evidence that it is. Many an adventurer has reached safety thanks to this small act of belief. On one memorable occasion I was greatly helped by choosing to believe things I considered totally untrue.

For the first half of my life, I gave weight only to facts, matter and physics, none of that woo-woo, spiritual stuff. I believed everything in the world consisted only of atoms and molecules. I thought that when we die we simply are no more and there is nothing. The way I saw it, after we stopped living, our atoms and molecules were recycled into other things and that was that. I didn't have any concept of a soul, a spirit or eternity. That was my staunch belief.

About four years after my mother died, I spent the day at a beautiful waterhole in the middle of nowhere, in the bush, in Australia. I was with my friend from

England and another young traveler we'd met along the way. We were bathing, talking and splashing in the glorious wildness, surrounded by red earth, ancient rocks and magnificent gum trees. In that afternoon sky, with the birds and cicadas, in the stillness and the wonder of it all, unexpectedly, I sensed my mother.

I'd not really grieved properly at the time she died, as I was focusing on supporting my distraught father. Time passed and my father seemed more settled, needing me less. When the opportunity for a one-year job in Australia presented itself, my thirst for new experiences made the choice easy. Leaving autumnal London one October my adventure began. Once the intended year was up, I decided to stay in this large, untamed country. The grief of losing my mother simmered, unattended, surfacing periodically, postponed.

And there, that day, in that place, I felt her. I saw and sensed her watching me, smiling, being happy for me, admiring the place I was in, the life I was living, expressing her affection and love without any sadness.

I didn't believe in any of that stuff; not a word of it. As far as I was concerned, it wasn't remotely true. I would have argued heatedly for my materialism. But in that moment what I did realise was that what I was sensing was *helpful*. It gave me comfort, and joy, it eased my grief, and almost blew it away. My grief was never the same again.

In that moment I made a very conscious choice. I saw the thought, the feeling, I named it as not true, I didn't believe it. Yet I also saw I liked it and I knew it was good. So I kept it. I kept the thought, I kept the allowance of my mother watching me, smiling at me and for me, being happy where she was and happy to see me where I was.

It's still with me, it's stayed ever since, it's been immensely helpful. It also started me on this journey of choosing what is helpful over what can be proven to be true by experiments and by researchers in laboratories who can never have the bigger picture precisely because they are in a laboratory.

Chapter 11
But It's Inauthentic

Popular culture is full of hints suggesting we would be flaky and fake if we were to change our opinions, beliefs, personality traits or even our wardrobe, but I question whether that is a useful message.

If a Tennessee-born actor masters the accents of a famous rapper, a British royal and a Scottish farmer, are they any less their true selves when they are speaking in those accents?

What about changing character? Johnny Depp is very different as Willy Wonka than he is as Jack Sparrow. Tom Cruise is very different in *Tropic Thunder* than he is in *Risky Business*. If actors must change not only their accent but also their entire character, then does this mean that for awhile they are no longer who they are?

You are probably quite different when you are with a group of friends on holiday than you are with your colleagues at work. When you are alone with your best friend, you are probably nothing like you'd be if you were talking with the person at the bank who says you can't access your funds. In all those varied situations, are you not still you?

Just because you behave differently in different situations does not mean you are being inauthentic, you are simply adapting to each environment. Our outward personality and behaviours, as well as our accent, can change and therefore can't define who we are.

How about our beliefs? Did you change who you were when you stopped believing in the tooth fairy?

Maybe your mother said you'd catch a cold if you went outdoors with wet hair and you believed her. Later you studied germ theory and concluded it was inhaling a virus that led to your colds, not wet hair. You changed your belief about colds, you did not change who you are. What will happen if you study something else in the future that leads you to believe that viruses aren't at all what you thought they were — will you hang on like grim death to a former belief regardless of what fascinating new insights you glean?

Our opinions are equally liable to change, if we are adaptive and continually evolving as nature intended. One particular political or religious persuasion may be just what you want for a period of time, but you are not wedded to your opinions for life. People change their politics or their religion for all sorts of reasons, some deep, some trivial, it need only make sense to the person doing the changing because they are the only one who can say what is right for them.

When you change the stories you live your life by, you are not being inauthentic or disloyal to your true self and you are not being fake or an impostor. You are being the adaptable, life-loving being you were born to be.

Who Are You?

So what is your true self?

I don't pretend to have a definitive answer to such a big philosophical question, but I'd suggest that what defines you is something beyond words and descriptions, just like a sunset is beyond words and descriptions.

Though personality traits exist in all of us, how you express them is unique to you. These traits are unique to you and they evolve over time. We are not supposed to be set in stone, fixed and immutable - that's called being dead.

You also have preferences which are unique to you. Even if everyone on earth had access to the exact same foods, career options, cars and clothes, you would still have your unique blend of things that attract you and things that don't.

The same is true of your values. We all have access to the same values —

things like freedom, courage, love and contribution — but we place different degrees of importance on those, and express them in different ways. Love can be expressed by being the best hairdresser, the best mother or the best artist that we can be. There are a gazillion ways to express our uniqueness and they cannot possibly stay the same throughout our whole life and in all situations.

You simply are you. Try that on for size. Try saying: "I am" with a full stop after it. Try taking away all your labels and descriptors. You don't cease to exist when you do that. You still feel the same, smell the same, look the same and love the same things. You're still you.

Just as a right-handed person has a perfectly functional left hand, our tendencies cannot define who we are. A right-handed person who loses their right arm does not become someone else once they have mastered doing everything with their left hand.

Similarly, an introverted person can learn to be extroverted, a pessimistic person can learn to be optimistic and a disorganised person can learn to be organised. They are still the same person. They can't be anyone else.

Personality tests, archetypes and astrological charts might provide fascinating insights and many people use such tools to guide their choices of partner or career. But tools are not meant to define us, constrain us or put us in a box. Personality traits evolve over your lifetime according to your mood, life stage or environment. That doesn't mean you will become a different person and it doesn't mean you were being a fake.

You will always have the same fingerprints and you will always be who you are. When you decide to change your stories and your behaviours in ways that make life more beautiful, this frees you to be of greater value. It's a life-enhancing act that benefits you and everyone around you. It frees you to follow your passions and your preferences and become even more the real you, never less.

Discarding The Outdated

Living in fear of being judged, criticised and accused of pretending to be something we're not keeps us small. Holding on for dear life to opinions, habits, stories and beliefs regardless of new desires and new intentions makes no sense.

Once we realise an opinion or belief is outdated, incomplete or downright silly, the constructive thing to do is to change our opinion or belief. And then, later on, change again!

Life is about new information, new perspectives and new circumstances. It's being willing to experiment, to try on different things and thus refine the art of being more and more true to who we really are.

Let's say you've spent your whole life believing that money is evil and then you have an epiphany that turns that thought on its head. Let's say you then see an opportunity to create an amazing life-enhancing project or business. Are you selling your soul to the devil if you admit that actually in some cases money can be used for great good?

Some of my happiest moments came from understanding I'd been wrong about something. When my boss at the sexual health clinic flicked off with his thumbnail a patch of dried blood from the penis of my terrified patient, I was delighted to discover my diagnosis of melanoma was entirely wrong.

On many other occasions I have found great freedom in the realisation I'd been mistakenly and unnecessarily bound to an old belief I was much better off without. A personal highlight was discovering that I was not automatically destined to die of bowel cancer at 61 as my mother had done simply because she was my mother and because I enjoy eating bacon.

I'll bet you've had a few of those welcome revelations too. Sometimes it's finding out our partner was not in fact cheating on us but planning a surprise party.

Even a magazine can benefit from the gift of having been mistaken. The cover of *TIME* magazine in 1999 declared that in fact eggs and cholesterol are not, after all, to be feared and avoided as they had proclaimed on their cover in 1984.

Being wrong is not the terrible thing it's portrayed to be. Being wrong is immensely empowering, not only because of the new perspective it reveals, but also because it is one more piece of proof that we are meant to evolve, to progress, to discard the unhelpful and embrace the more helpful.

You cannot lose or diminish your true authentic self. When you allow yourself the balm of swapping out old stories for ones you craft yourself purely because they make you feel good, your true self only gets clearer and brighter.

Chapter 12
Taking Action

At this juncture you may be wondering about how best to put some of these concepts into practice. After all, experience is a much more powerful teacher than words on a page.

While you were reading, you probably formed quite a few ideas on how you might go ahead with changing some of your stories — all those ideas will be beneficial, so giving them a try is an excellent way to proceed. I would encourage you to experiment will any and all the ideas my book may have sparked in you about how you might apply its principles in your own personal life. This will be far more effective than any prescriptions I or anyone else could give you as they will take into account your own preferences, experiences and level of understanding.

It is also useful to clarify the process by identifying the key elements that lead to unveiling your stories and starting to reframe those you believe are not serving you or to craft new ones. I will outline the steps below.

Awareness

The first element is to notice the stories, to become aware of them. This is as simple as paying attention to how you are feeling. For example, if you are going about your day and you start to notice that you feel tense, your movements are stiff and your voice is constricted, or you experience other physical signs of emotion such as shallow breathing or a knot in your stomach, then there's a story going on. Noticing, all on its own, is important progress, even if you are too busy in that moment to do anything more than that. This is because every step towards changing your stories builds on previous steps and gives you a lived experience that you are doing something to change and that change is safe. So becoming a good noticer, becoming better and better at catching yourself in the act of getting hooked, is an excellent skill to aim for.

Observation

After the initial awareness, add depth to that awareness by calmly observing the *sensory* experience of what it is to be hooked by a story. This involves noting your sensations, emotions and thoughts and letting yourself experience them with curiosity rather than resistance, with interest rather than judgement. It might go something like this:

Sensations: tight throat, hunched upper back, stiff movements;

Emotions: fear, insecurity, dread;

Thoughts: *I'll never get this finished today, what am I going to do?*

Remember, you are not doing anything about it, you are only observing. You are like a reporter or a field worker, taking note of what is there but you have no opinion of it.

Uncovering

The next step is to do a bit of gentle detective work as to what beliefs underlie the thoughts that led to the emotions and what story is associated with those beliefs. Use the examples in this book as inspiration, as well as examples from your own life. The 12 unhelpful stories in Chapter 4 may help you identify what narratives are operating. Do not expect to uncover everything immediately. This is more of an onion-peeling process you will do gradually over many iterations. You can ask yourself: "For me to have those thoughts, what must I believe?" For example, if you are anxious that you won't finish a task today, you may believe that somebody else's opinion of you carries more weight than your own. Or it might be that you believe you are only of value if you complete all tasks to a set schedule. Don't try to force these insights, rather allow them to arrive in their own time. Forcing this process can make it feel like a chore and inhibit your intuition. If nothing comes to you today, that's fine, just try again next time.

Questioning

Gently probe the snippets of beliefs, assumptions, perceptions and stories that you do uncover. *Is that true? Is it helpful to see it this way? What's another way to look at it? How will this situation seem to me in 5 years? How might the other person be feeling? What might their perspective look like? Am I jumping to conclusions? What conclusions, and why am I jumping to them? Can I observe this as if I were a curious Martian with nothing at stake? Why does this feel so important to me? Could I see it as less important, or important in different ways?*

Finding Better Thoughts

Now create new statements, new thoughts, new ideas and new ways to look at the topic. Instead of *I can't pay my bills,* try out *I made it work somehow last time.* Instead of *I feel so alone* try out I *do quite often enjoy me-time, especially when I go for a walk.* From your original thought, create a different statement around that topic. Then check in with how you feel when you make the new statement. If you feel worse or the same, find another statement. Look for statements that make you feel better, just a little bit. Keep coming up with statements about this topic until you can feel your emotional state shift to a better-feeling, more empowered, more light-hearted one. Even a tiny shift in that direction is to be celebrated. If you start off feeling hopeless and you shift to feeling resentful, that might not sound like progress, but it is, because resentment is a more powerful state than hopelessness. From this tiny shift, try for another tiny shift in that better direction. Resentful could become angry and then motivated, this increases your feeling of power and decreases your feeling of helplessness, you're going in the right direction. It's not that you're going to stay stuck in anger, it's that anger is a stepping stone between helpless and motivated. If finding a better thought right now on this topic is just too hard, and sometimes it will be, because the topic may be highly charged, then make statements about different topics, still with the aim of finding a better feeling. When you find that better feeling, even if it's only a little bit better, milk it. Stay in it, bask in it, savour it and pay attention to the way you feel, revel in the improved sensations, however small the improvement. Don't be looking for a dramatic, miraculous transformation, don't expect to move from the pit of despair to nirvana in one jump. Simply look for a tangible shift into a slightly better feeling. Some days you will feel a bigger shift, other days it will be subtle. All shifts are progress, all shifts change your biochemistry, your neurology, your wellbeing and contribute to that better future.

Patient Repetition

Rome wasn't built in a day. Changing your stories is like getting a muscular body, it doesn't happen with a couple of weight-lifting sessions. But it does happen, it can't not happen, if you approach the process with patience, consistency, trust in your own success and with a willingness to repeatedly, doggedly keep having a go. The other attitudes that will help immeasurably are to keep it light, not letting it become a burden and to accept as normal that there will be days when you feel frustrated, defeated, irritated and want to throw in the towel. The good news about those days is that it is precisely when we feel like giving up that we are learning the most and that a mini-breakthrough is due. Sometimes you'll get a big aha, something will visibly change and you'll feel immediately freer, but most of the time your progress will be incremental but nevertheless significant. Try to notice all your wins, big or small, because by doing that you are making the next win come sooner.

Stay On Target And Keep It Simple

When you are learning something and it feels important, it's easy to get distracted and taken off course by a new guru, technique, explanation or lifestyle hack. Keep it simple. There may be value in the shiny new thing, but it could also take you off course. Modern culture tells the story that being able to quote studies and research, being able to explain our problem in terms of complex, intricate, sciency-sounding terminology, rigorously implementing the protocol of the guru — that these are the ways to progress. It's not that those things are necessarily bad things, but it pays to keep an eye on the mindset that comes along with them. If you find yourself overthinking, over-analysing, obsessing over the minutiae, making rigid rules, huffing and puffing to keep up with the latest... then you may want to come back to basics. What are the basics? They are: *I am uniquely me. I am living my life in the best way I know how. I am always learning. I am doing great.*

Support Measures

You can support the process of story-reframing by making sure to get plenty of fun, play and especially laughter. Watch comedy shows on YouTube, find what's hilarious about the day you just had (there's always something) or laugh for no reason at all. Laughter increases your supply of happy hormones (dopamine, serotonin, endorphins and oxytocin) and keeps the stress hormones (noradrenaline, adrenaline and cortisol) in check. It has many other physiological benefits but the best reason to laugh is because it makes you feel great, and after all, why else are we even talking about any of this, if not because we want to feel great?

Aside from laughter, time in nature nurtures you and aids in regaining perspective. This can be listening to birdsong and other nature sounds, gazing at the sky, tree canopy or a body of water, feeling the wind on your face and the sand or earth beneath your feet. If you are in a high-rise in a big city even looking out the window, at an indoor plant or an image from nature will still soothe your system.

Doing kind things for yourself, speaking to yourself nicely, smiling to and at yourself, saying nice things to yourself in the mirror, stroking your own arms and face and giving yourself praise will probably feel extremely weird if you're not used to doing that, but if you let it, it will amuse you and cheer you. Those are states that greatly support you in living and breathing better stories.

First Aid Measures

In the heat of the moment, when a story grabs you, it may be hard to do all the calm and measured things I'm suggesting. You're feeling strong emotions, you're neither calm nor measured. In this case, your best bet is distraction. There are a million ways to distract yourself. Watch something on TV, change the subject, sing a song, run around the block, go shopping, clean the bathroom, listen to a podcast, put some soothing music on, dance, do a workout… There's nothing wrong with distraction! If it takes your mind off the story, it's helping to settle you, it's reducing your stress hormones and it's giving you a breather. This is not the same as hiding or suppressing your emotions. You're not hiding or suppressing anything when you distract yourself, on the contrary. You're recognising that you feel agitated with uncomfortable feelings and you're boldly choosing to do something to try to feel better.

Pitfalls

Sometimes it's tempting to dive headlong into the story in the belief that we can get to the bottom of it and fix it or extinguish it at last. Too often, we only end up wallowing in it and augmenting all the negative emotions and their accompanying stress hormones. A quick insight, a quick realisation about the origin of the story may come to you and that's all you need. You don't need to compulsively follow that thought in a vain attempt to arrive at *The Answer*. There is no *The Answer*. You don't need to know the exact origin of your story to be able to create better ones. I've given you examples, in this book, of stories with an origin. For instance, I pieced together what I thought was the reason I reacted with so much stress to the email from my accountant. But that is only my extrapolation, my best guess. To me it's entertaining and intellectually satisfying to piece together what I think happened and why. However it's not necessary. And for all I know, my explanation may be wrong. By all means, if finding a root explanation for your story pleases you the way it pleases me, then do the Sherlock Holmes thing. But with or without that root cause, you can still easily figure out which beliefs you want to change and go ahead and change them.

Another pitfall is the habit many of us have of chastising ourselves, of running a punitive and critical narrative over the top of the story that's hooked us. This secondary narrative says we're an idiot for feeling this way, for being hooked by these emotions. It says we're weak and may call us names. Or it may place the blame on others and shower them with our wrath. That's not going to help either. You're in a story, it's ok, you didn't do anything wrong and it's not someone's fault, but nor are you going to let yourself stay hooked. What you're going to do, life-loving soul that you are, is take action by removing yourself altogether from the story. That's what the *constructive* use of distraction achieves.

Distraction doesn't always help. There's nothing that *always* helps. We can only do the best we can in the moment. There will be times when you are in full fight-or-flight mode, fully immersed in a story that's got you hooked and there is just nothing you can do to stop it. That's ok. It will happen from time to time. It's only natural. Never beat yourself up if this happens, just accept you're on a runaway train — it will be over soon! Your story, no matter how intense, will spend itself, will wear itself out. It will lose momentum and grind to a halt, they always do. When it does, you get to rest, recover, take a deep breath and try again tomorrow. A nap, a walk or a chat with a friend may get you back on track, but it may not. Sometimes you just can't get away and you have to sit it out. It's normal. Think of it as you would think of being caught in the rain without an umbrella. It's cold, it's unpleasant, but it doesn't keep raining forever.

Some stories and situations are convoluted and prolonged. Some may drag on for weeks and all you can do is grin and bear it. You can bear it, and you can remain true to your intention throughout it all and wait for the clouds to part and the story to shift. If you keep your aim on looking for the better thought, picturing the better future, shifting to the more helpful story, you will get there.

Applying the principles in this chapter will enable you to transform any story you deem unhelpful into an uplifting story. In the next chapter we will explore another essential element for shifting your less enjoyable stories to ones that make you feel amazing.

Chapter 13
Words Tell Your Story

The *content* of a story is not the only element with impact. The specific *words* we use to tell it also have their effect. Let's return one last time to Richard and Sarah in order to illustrate this and give you a felt experience of the power of words to evoke feelings. As you read, take note of what thoughts and feelings come to you.

The Princess And The Prince

Once upon a time, there lived a fairy princess in a kingdom of alpine mountains, flower-strewn meadows, fresh air and the most amazingly delicious cherries. The young princess would eat the cherries as she climbed the trees with her friends. She knew she was the princess of a beautiful, amazing kingdom and she also knew that it was her destiny to one day leave the kingdom to explore far and wide, for her heart yearned for adventure.

In another kingdom far away lived a prince. He was a keen observer and a thoughtful witness and in his kingdom there was war. His brave and much-loved parents, the king and queen, kept him back from the actual fighting, but he saw firsthand the destructive effects of the conflict. He saw how it hurt his parents and the people, how it diminished and drained their reserves. He decided to make it his life's work to understand conflict and how differences between people could be more harmoniously managed.

As this prince and princess went about their individual missions, knowing nothing of each other, they experienced many romances with other princesses and princes. Then came the magical moment when they met. They were perfect for each other. What each sought was in the other; the mysteries they wished to uncover and the experiences they wished to embody came easily when they were together. At first it was a whirlwind of excitement, a thrilling adventure. They felt electrified by the discovery in each other and in themselves of so much understanding, such clear vision and so much potential.

The energy of their togetherness led to the birth of a new being, a baby boy, a new miracle of uniqueness, the blending of two great powers and a whole new power in his own right.

The miracle of the baby son brought more joy to the prince and the princess than either of them could have imagined. It also brought them a new clarity. What became clear to them was that the magic they had made together, just like the magic of their early years, was transforming into a new phase in their lives. It would soon be time for their relationship to come to a close and for a different connection to emerge. They saw that the spells that had been cast on their innocent loving parents were playing out in their own lives and they understood they were now to part ways and go forth individually.

The sadness of parting mingled in their hearts with a liberating relief and a soaring desire to continue the thrilling adventure of life in their own unique and separate ways. Although they were now apart, they continued always to share a delight at the blossoming of their son and both understood that this son they had together given life to was their teacher as much as he was their student.

In this new phase of their solo adventures and their life-long quest for learning they both found much joy. Each evolved to higher levels of being. Some lessons were painful and others delightful but all led to expansion of their consciousnesses. They watched with wonder the same take place in their son and saw into the future a long line of joyful beings perpetually evolving in marvellous ways.

Today they continue forth, needing nothing from each other, grateful for all the lessons, gifts and insights they gave each other, delighting in the continuance of a life of fun, adventure and fulfilment in their own very different ways.

Perspective Matters

You may have found this last story cheesy, romantic or anything in between, but did it engender different emotions than the other versions? You're familiar now with some different angles on the Sarah and Richard story and you could create more, if you felt like it.

I often wonder, when reading about Genghis Khan, Napoleon or any historical figure we think we know everything about, what their story would be like if it were told by their mother, their enemy, their childhood best friend, their dog or their fairy godmother.

How you tell your story matters. Words carry emotional charge and words paint pictures. The images and the feelings that accompany the facts of your story have a huge effect on how you perceive the events of your life, how you see yourself and by extension, what is true for you right now and into the future.

To experience the power of words, I invite you to try the following activity. As you read the words below, taken from this and the other accounts of Sarah and Richard's tale, take note of where you smile and feel uplifted, or where you frown and feel dragged down. Notice what mental images pop into your head.

Fairy princess; alpine mountains; flower-strewn meadows; fresh air; amazingly delicious cherries; kingdom; beautiful; explore far and wide; prince; keen observer; much-loved; decided; life's work; managed better; miracle; baby son; joy; imagined; clarity; magic; transforming; connection; innocent; go forth; thrilling adventure of life; blossoming; this new phase; quest for learning; perpetually evolving; gifts and insights; continuance; a life of fun.

How did you feel? What concepts, sensations and ideas sparked and formed themselves in your mind? Now read this next list, taken from the version in Chapter 2:

Passive-aggressive; playful; judgemental; badger people into listening; no idea; Celtic warriors; troublesome burden; beleaguered; disappeared off the scene; turbulent home; might be wanted; mundane; thrilling; happy-ever-after; needy; adventures; unsettle; blamed; surly; retaliated; strangely familiar; being "right"; moral high ground; lit up in joy; seething with resentment; hopeless; victim; heartless; unhelpful narratives; miraculously; survival instincts; dissolved; painful.

On reading this list, what was your experience, emotionally and in terms of the mental images it conjured? The final two lists come from Chapter 6. Notice how you feel when you skim through them.

Didn't work out; bloody passive-aggressive; incredibly annoying; wheedle or whine; slam doors; pitiful; feisty; intimidated; all front; harridan; never happy; pissed off; gone out of her; slam doors; sarcastic things; gave up trying; snivelling; just an act; disillusioned; expecting the world; done with that; always; manipulative; got my own back; stew in her own sourness; should have been.

Men are bastards; harsh; I should know; selfish abusive men; had me hooked; surly, superior, domineering; cheat, lie, steal; users; how nice they seem; selfish lazy teenagers; typical; thought he was going to be different; stupid me; showed his true colours; told him straight; selfish disrespectful behaviour; be treated this way; no way; drinking and carousing; everything on my own; sent him packing; just weak.

What emotions and visuals came up this time?

Answers will of course vary widely. We each have our own individual take on how a particular word affects us, depending on our own history. We also vary as to how sensitive we are to the emotional effect of words. Nonetheless, the activity gives you a sense that when you do tell a story about what happened in your life, the words you choose will powerfully affect how your story is perceived, what emotions it engenders, what picture of you and the world it paints.

When you tell your stories you are painting your reality. You are creating an image of your past, your present and your future. You are influencing how you see yourself, how others see you, how you feel about life and how you relate to people. Your words are creating your reality because how you feel and how you view yourself and the world is part of your reality.

If you want to create a life you love, you can do so by your choice of what stories you tell and the words you use to tell them. Words that convey woe, doom, injustice and abuse paint a picture of your life that may not be the one you want to live. The facts of your story may all be correct, your story may indeed be one of woe, doom, injustice and abuse, but the way you tell it will be what determines your present reality. You can choose the way you tell that story, even when it's based on the same facts.

Let's put that skill into practice! I'm going to invite you to apply this to one of your own stories, so let's choose a suitable one to start. It should be familiar and not highly charged emotionally.

What do you say when someone asks you where you come from, or where you grew up? Are you often asked how you met your partner, or how you broke up? Or maybe how you got your job, bought your house, started your business? Pick a story that you often tell, that you tell without really thinking about it. Maybe you have a funny story about the time you were in Morocco or the thing that happened on the way to work one day.

How do you tell that story? What would you say if you were telling it right now? Record yourself relating the story out loud, exactly as you would if someone really asked you. Keep it to about 2 - 3 minutes.

Listen to your recording (or, if you didn't record it, recall what you said) looking for the words or phrases that stand out to you and note how they feel for you.

Now turn your attention to the facts. The facts are all the elements which nobody could deny took place if they had witnessed the event. The facts are not open to interpretation. Write a list of the facts, being careful to avoid words like abandoned, betrayed, lied to, criticised, humiliated or cheated — these are interpretations, not facts. The facts are what any uninvolved person would observe if they saw a video recording or transcript of the event, with no evaluation as to what was intended or meant.

Look at your list of facts as if you were someone else, someone who hasn't lived the story, who knows nothing about it and has access to nothing but this list of bare naked facts. Now tell your story aloud, recording it if possible, telling of those same facts but using completely novel phrases, tone and ideas. Approach is as if you truly had no recollection of the event.

This may be easier if you don a character, pretending you are Mr Spock from *Star Trek*. Or you could be a script-writer creating a sit-com, a documentary or a kids' cartoon. Be creative, pick a different historical era, go for a comedic twist or make it a high drama.

Listen to your recording of this second version of the story, or recall what you said. How do you feel? What stands out? How do the feelings and perceptions differ from the first rendition?

I invite you to come back to this exercise, to do this as many times as you like, finding novel and varied ways to relate the same facts. Have fun with it, let it provide a playful perspective on how mutable stories are. Try it on a few different stories and then when you're up for it, gently try it on more emotionally charged stories. If it feels too confronting, then just back down to a safer story and try again later with the more difficult one.

Try different accents, different ages and genders, different costumes and physical features. If there's a young woman in the story, turn her into an elderly man or a famous opera singer. Make the villain the hero and vice versa, have a fairytale version or make it a musical. You could imitate Jane Austen or Shakespeare. Set it in a forest in the Congo, a beach in Guatemala or a mediaeval castle in Austria.

Doing this will give you all the tools you need to rewrite all the stories in your life, all the ones you want to rewrite, that is. You don't need fancy exercises, strict methodologies or decades of psychoanalysis (unless you enjoy those things). You can play with this process and come back to it as many times as you wish, each time refining and embellishing your skills at telling the stories you want to live by and being the author of your own life.

I know this sounds ridiculously simple and it is. Most helpful things are. The secret is to keep doing it and keep playing at it. Repetition and playfulness are the two key ingredients of success at learning and success at refining patterns of thought and action.

Now you have a felt experience of what it's like to live in a different story. This is phenomenal because it proves to your system that change is safe, possible and fun. It's letting you feel lighter and less bound up in your existing stories. It's showing you the path to freedom.

Your instinct is to choose what feels best as long as it feels safe. Doing this activity regularly proves to your unconscious mind that new stories are safe, that nothing bad happens when you loosen your grip on the old story.

Little by little, softly, your unconscious mind will come around. It will figure out that it's okay to do this and then it will start to do it automatically, without you needing to direct the show. You are resetting your autopilot to happy.

Happy is a good place to be, especially when you realise what gifts your stories have been bringing you all along, even those pesky unhelpful ones. This is what chapter 14 is about.

Chapter 14

Stories Bring Gifts

As you move forward in your journey and look to the future, it's important to know that none of your stories have been wasted. They are not bad, wrong or nasty. Even unhelpful stories have benefited you in some way.

Along with their unhelpful aspects, each story has nevertheless shaped you in a positive way as well. They have made you who you are, they have been with you on your path. Your stories can be seen as a blessing! I know that throughout this book I have shown you the ways in which our stories may hinder us but that is only because we tend to get stuck in them and forget to create more relevant stories for who we are becoming.

Even the stories you no longer need or want, which are not serving you any longer, did bring you some blessings. There are three valuable gifts you have received from your stories.

Gift 1: Survival

Your first stories were crafted from when you were very young. You were small then and physically helpless. Your parents or caregivers had their own stuff going on. You needed their care and you needed to do whatever it took to get that care. Small and helpless though you were, you were a capable young thing. On an unconscious level, you knew what you needed to do, think and believe to get the love and acceptance, the care and nurturance, your survival depended on. You did that and you did it well, that's why you survived.

I don't know if you had loving, kind parents or abusive, narcissistic parents or anything in between. Whatever your parents' intentions, it's likely they had their own backstories with feelings of unworthiness and a need for outside validation. Once they had you, they wanted to shield themselves from judgement and criticism others might express about your appearance or behaviour. If they took it out on you it's probably because they didn't know what else to do to gain the approval they thought they needed to survive, whether it was approval from their family, neighbours or their own inner voice. It's a rare parent who doesn't worry, at least a little bit, that their child's looks and actions reflect on them.

You understood that in order to keep their love and acceptance and therefore survive, and in order to manage that in the face of your own evolving wants, then you would need to do whatever you needed to do. You learned by trial and error. You did your best to balance what you needed and what you had to do to have those needs met by your parents or caregivers. Sometimes that meant compliance and agreement and at other times, especially as you grew more independent, it may have meant doing all the things they didn't approve of and didn't want you to do, because there are many ways to achieve the same aims. Whatever strategy you chose, whatever you did, it worked, you survived. Job well done.

Gift 2: Purpose

During all you have lived through, you have learned about what you like and don't like. You have been presented with situations, environments and life events that have led you to know more clearly what you want and don't want. Your emotions have made that clear to you. When you felt frustrated, angry or sad, you were learning to distinguish between what in life you want to pursue and what you want to move away from. This is priceless information.

Your life stories have revealed your uniqueness, your path. We are all made up of the same basic elements, just as a painting is made up of the same primary colours. We want to feel good, we want to feel happy, we want to know love, acceptance and beauty. We want healthy strong bodies and we want to freely express ourselves. We want a good life.

There are an infinity of ways we can have that good life! Just as no two paintings are alike, even though they're painted with the same primary colours, no two happy lives are alike.

So while we all have the same desires to feel good, to be of value, to be all we can be, the specific ways in which we embody that will be completely unique to us.

I met a man who expressed his unique and joyful self through spending his entire life being a happily married barber in a small town and loving every minute of his life. The story of his life manifested that way and it gave him joy. Others express themselves and find happiness through building an empire or sailing solo around the world. The specific physical ways in which you pursue your values and desires have been informed by the stories you have held through your life.

Your stories are your launchpad to create a life you love. Stories point you in the right direction. It's uncomfortable when they do that, because they show us what we like by presenting us with what we intensely dislike so that we may experience the contrast required to make our choice. However, the discomfort can be transient if we use that knowledge to pursue and create all the things we do like.

Gift 3: Superpowers

Each of those stories, for all its unhelpful aspects, also carries an antidote, which can become a superpower. One person's story may have them feeling angry about injustice, allowing them to learn they are passionate about creating more justice. Another person's story may have them feeling weak and incapable and this leads them to a love of physical fitness and expressing themselves that way.

Check in your memory bank and see where you have excelled in your life purely because you deliberately were changing a story about you that you didn't want to keep. If you grew up believing yourself to be inept, you have likely become adept or even masterful at something. If you grew up feeling unworthy, you may have gone out of your way to be the thoughtful one.

Perhaps you're amazing at baking cakes, delivering speeches, or writing poetry. You might excel at sculpture or real estate investing or you might host the best parties or knit the best scarves. It might be something grandiose or something so simple it's overlooked, but because of your story, because it showed you what you don't want to feel and you pursued what you do want to feel, you have developed special abilities and skills that bring joy to you and others.

We all have superpowers, and they arose from our stories of lack. Our stories gave us our superpowers. You may be reluctant to give yourself credit for your superpowers, or areas of mastery may be hidden from you right now. But they're there.

What's Next?

I've been writing about stories that keep us trapped, small and unhappy. But stories don't have to do that. They do that when we stay stuck in them and when we give some parts of the story too much weight, and other parts too little weight. Stories only keep us stuck when we get hooked by certain emotions and don't find our way back out the other side.

When we live and tell our stories we can get way-laid among the weeds and forget to move on to the happy ending. Let's not do that, let's use our stories as a trampoline that propels us towards our purpose and our superpowers. We can kiss old stories goodbye and eagerly make new ones to fit where we are today, not where we were back then.

Every story you have ever told about yourself or ever believed to be true has gifts that can be appreciated and celebrated. The reason to reframe or remove old stories is not because they are bad, evil and dangerous. The reason to create and refine new stories is not because they are right, good and virtuous.

The reasons are simply that life is not meant to be static, we are not meant to be stuck in an outdated story any more than we are meant to stay still and never move.

We can let go of stories, habits, beliefs and attitudes that are outdated and past their best. We need to do that if we want to be expanding our horizons and building a life we love. The old stories served their purpose, they did a good job and we can be grateful for what they taught us even as we let them go.

Now we are free to look around and ask: "What's next?" What can I look forward to with eagerness and pleasurable anticipation, what can I create, what can I build, what can I experience that will be fun and exciting? That is what being the author of your own life is all about.

Conclusion

So what can you look forward to if you implement the ideas in this book?

You can look forward to more of what you want, whatever that may be. You may want to live in a Caribbean tax haven and sip champagne at sundown on the deck of your yacht. You may want a cabin in the woods next to a spring-fed creek, falling asleep to the sound of kookaburras. Infinite visions exist and yours may be still gestating, but underneath all the possible visions I believe we all want the same very simple things: a good life, the love of good people, wellness, vitality and to feel good.

You can have those things with or without lots of money, with or without a yacht, a cabin in the woods or any kookaburras. How? By taking the reins. Not the huffing and puffing and trying harder reins, but the reins of what you allow yourself to think about, what images you choose to display in your mind's eye, what words you select to describe your challenges and desires and what feelings you give airtime to. You can move away from old patterns that keep you stuck and move towards patterns that take you forward to that life, however it may look in its specific details.

The long and the short of it is: stories just beneath our awareness run our lives. We got them in childhood from our environment, just as nature intended. We got more throughout our lives and they built on each other. As we grew up, we forgot to audit them for usefulness and so we are still running on a few that are well past their best-by date. We are all innately capable of identifying unhelpful narratives and beliefs, and using our attention and creativity to modify some, discard others and create better ones. This will lead to our living happier, longer and more healthful lives. It takes some patience and focused attention but it's not rocket science. Nobody is forcing you to do any of this, but if you want to do it, don't use the excuse that you can't or it's too hard, just go for it. Use the ideas in this book and any other ideas you pick up, but primarily do it your own way - you're you. If you don't like what I've said, good, you're you, but just make sure that you're disliking it authentically and not from some outdated story. Write your own story and live your own life and don't let anyone tell you how to live. Oh, and have fun, it's the real reason you're here in the first place.

There. You didn't really need to read a whole book. That's all I was trying to say.

I wish you well on your journey. With the right stories, every day from this day forth can be the best day of your life.

About The Author

Doris Hasslocher is a somewhat nomadic constant learner and experimenter with an ever-expanding and eclectic assortment of interests.

After enjoyable decades earning her keep from being a medical doctor in 3 countries and several specialties, she realised she also liked writing, coaching, making kefir, marketing, and learning more languages. She quit medicine to throw herself with gusto into those pursuits and to uncover more eclectic interests. When she has a free moment she likes to climb trees or walk barefoot in woods and on beaches.

As the mother of a handsome, healthy and accomplished young man, Doris doesn't take all the credit as that goes largely to the young man himself. In her parenting journey, Doris was assisted by a delightfully collaborative co-parent, two cats, a super-dog, some guinea pigs, a handful of chickens and a tribe of amazing humans.

Her online coaching business brings her joy and fulfilment as she guides and accompanies others in navigating choppy waters while learning to tell themselves stories of adventure, love and chocolate ice cream.

Doris is a firm believer in looking on the bright side and doing what feels right and trusting her instincts. Although she frequently falls short of her own expectations, she's very forgiving and quick to get back on the horse. She believes we all have the ability to be everything we want to be and she'll spread her message as far and wide as her technological and organisational skills allow.

She's not sure where exactly she lives as she is generally on the move, but countries she has lived in for more than 4 months include Australia, the

UK, Switzerland, South Africa, El Salvador, Mexico, Brazil, Indonesia and Germany, in no particular order.

UK, Switzerland, South Africa, El Salvador, Mexico, Brazil, Indonesia and Germany, in no particular order.

www.ingramcontent.com/pod-product-compliance
Lightning Source LLC
Chambersburg PA
CBHW071337140726
47996CB00005B/2014